The Fire
in These Ashes

A *Spirituality of Contemporary Religious Life*

Joan Chittister, OSB

Sheed & Ward
Kansas City

Sheed & Ward™ is a service of The National Catholic Reporter Publishing Company.

◆

Library of Congress Cataloguing-in-Publication Data

Chittister, Joan.
   The fire in these ashes : a spirituality of contemporary religious life / Joan Chittister.
        p.   cm.
    ISBN: 1-55612-802-9 (pbk. : alk. paper)
    1. Monastic and religious life. 2. Spirituality—Catholic Church.   I. Title.
   BX2435.C482   1995
   255—dc20   95-38415
                                                                    CIP

◆

Fourth printing, 1996.

Published by: Sheed & Ward
                    115 E. Armour Blvd.
                    P.O. Box 419492
                    Kansas City, MO 64141-6492

To order, call: (800) 333-7373

Cover design by Gloria Ortiz.

Contents

Acknowledgements

A number of people have been part of the thinking upon which this book is based. Some of them have shaped it by living the life extraordinarily well in a time when a criteria for making that judgment has been apparently blurred. Others have reflected out loud with me over the years about its ongoing development despite all the pressures and problems of the present age. Many have contributed by simply raising questions and fears and worries that emerge in a time of great change. A few have helped me by acting as Devil's Advocates and challenging the very existence of religious life at all. I am grateful to all of them for pressing me to find present value in a lifestyle that has lost the aura of a golden age and doubts the possibility of a future one.

Most of all, I am grateful to the people who took the time to read this manuscript out of the filter of their own lives and shared with me the editorial questions, concerns and comments that, as a result, enabled me to strengthen the text. Those people are: Marlene Bertke, OSB, Stephanie Campbell, OSB, Margarita Dangel, OSB, Mary Lee Farrell, GNSH, Augusta Hamel, OSB, Mary Lou Kownacki, OSB, Mary Rita Kuhn, SSJ, Anne McCarthy, OSB, Mary Miller, OSB, Julia Upton, RSM, Linda Romey, OSB, Christine Vladimiroff, OSB, Gail Grossman-Freyne and Brother Thomas Bezanson. To my peril, I may not have taken every suggestion but I definitely considered each one of them seriously.

I am, as always, particularly grateful to Marlene Bertke, OSB and Mary Grace Hanes, OSB who bring every manuscript of mine to the point of the professional. Most of all, I am grateful to Maureen Tobin, OSB for her continuing ability to give my life a semblance of normalcy while I continue to disrupt it by attempting to write while I attempt to go on living.

I am, in addition, deeply grateful to Tim and Christine O'Neil of Dublin, Ireland who provided me with the gift of the private space it takes for me to write a concentrated work.

This has been a good book for me to write. My only hope is that it will provide in others the thinking that it has in me.

*This book is dedicated
to Maureen Tobin, OSB,
mentor and friend,
in whose life I have seen the spirituality
that makes these words true.*

Preface

The world that spawned religious life, even the religious life of this century, is not the world we're living in. If religious life has anything to do with real life, the hope of recasting it in old molds smacks of pure fantasy. Spending time and energy yearning for the return of the mythical past while the present swirls perilously around us, awash in the debris of rationalism in the social order and dogmatism in the church, only holds us back, I think, from moving in holy ways in a post-modern world. Just as medievalism fell to scientific modernism, modernity is giving way to globalism. In both instances, the assumptions about reality and the world view of the past have proven inadequate to the conditions and findings of the present. Old images of God, old theological formulations of truth, old models of relationship, old concepts of human, civil, animal and natural rights buckle under the pressure. To cling even to the present, let alone the past, in such a time in history is simply to confuse the vision and make the present bleak. Not uncommonly, too, it divides groups and drains them of energy that should be being put into living well today.

The opposite temptation brings with it just as much danger, however. To attempt to fabricate a vision of religious life for a world we do not know, and for a time we may never see, takes as much power out of the present as a nostalgic commitment to the past. What's more, the fabrication, I think, is not for us to make. That is the work of the people who will live it. Our task is to live this time now, our time, well so that a future model can rise from these ashes with confidence and with courage.

The question is how to do that. Religious in large numbers are growing daily more disillusioned by endless historical review of past forms of religious life and long excursions into futuristic speculation, as well. They want to know if there is anything going on now to prove that religious life remains worth the ongoing sacrifice of their own lives. Is there anything still life-giving here? Is there anything yet valuable enough to go on doing here? New members want to know if there is anything here that merits their coming to do, their coming to be. Lay people want to know what religious life is all about today. Whatever they thought of cloister and habits and schedules and convent customs before, at least they knew what religious life was about. Now, they are not so sure anymore.

Everyday, thoughtful religious face or wrestle with the really current questions in religious life: Am I wasting my life to stay in such a place? Should anyone even dare to think of entering? What is the spiritual substance of religious life? Is there any spiritual substance left? Is religious life dying or rising or both? The questions are real. The temptation is to answer them out of either the past models or future imaginings. The truth of the answer is obvious and painful, apparent and exciting at the same time: There is only one place that is holy and that place is the here and now.

This book is about religious life in the here and now, not about the value of its past and not about the possible shape of its future. It asks a simple question: What, if anything, constitutes the spirituality of contemporary religious life? What is holy-making now? What is the work of religious life now? What are the virtues demanded of religious now that take character and test commitment, that make the world closer to the reign of God and a person closer to the Truth of life?

I'd love to say that I just thought all of this up. It would seem so creative, so fresh. As a matter of fact, however, this book has been in process in me for over 30 years. During this period of my own life, I have watched religious life both from an intensely personal position and from an internationally public perspective, both from the bottom of the institutional ladder and, like Simon Stylites, from the top of it, as a young nun before Vatican II and as a national administrator in the decades following it. I have watched it close-up in convents from Washington to Rome, from coast to coast, from Erie, Pennsylvania to Australia and back. I have chaired and presided and interviewed and organized and researched religious life through phase after phase of the renewal project. As a communication theorist and social scientist, I looked always for signs of life and signs of holiness, asked myself what, if anything, was bringing life to religious communities, despite the struggles of change, and what was not. This book is my accumulation of answers to those questions.

I would love to say, too, that this work contains a blueprint for the future. And in a sense, it does – but only for those who recognize the future in the present. Seasoned members need to redefine the spiritual disciplines of their lives, to recognize that the asceticisms of the life may have changed but the character and quality of the life have not changed a bit. They must suspect the retreat to commitment – the desperate clinging to the old forms of religious life simply because they do not recognize its new ones and remember the past as a quieter place – and come to see what commitment really demands of them now. Newer members need to realize that what they are working with in communities today are not all signs of decline; they are often new life in the making.

They must resist the retreat to the romantic. They must not be frightened by uncertainty or depressed by smallness. They must be able to see the great energy of the process. They must choose their spiritual vision well, not from the ashes of the glorious past, not from the dream of a glorious future, but from the challenges of the present. "Choose God, not where God lives," the Desert Monastics teach us. Don't wish your life away. There is work to be done in this period, Mystery to be lived in this period, that is essential to the conflagration of the Spirit in our times. After all, religious life is not the only institution in the world that is aging, in the midst of change, open to speculation, in need of new energy, and in hope of new vision. After going through 25 years of social transformation, religious can have a great gift to bring to the process of change in other groups, in the church as well as in the public arena, if they can only articulate it.

Though I honestly believe that the configuration of contemporary spiritual ideals developed in this work may well serve any type of religious community, vowed or not, celibate or not – whatever its type or composition or mission – this book does not pretend to be about new forms of religious life. This book is about the holiness required, the burning sanctity involved, in living this one, the one that is in-between the respected old and the emerging new, the one that is pioneering, the one that is in process in a world reeling from the permanency of change at a step-over moment in history.

This book, in other words, is meant to be a word of soul to those who carry the vision of religious life during this time – young and old, newer or older members – and who seek to rethink its purpose, its blessings and its power in a period when it has become more fashionable to speak of its demise than its resurrection.

The book's theme and title derives from the Gaelic process of *grieshog*, of keeping old fires alive for the sake of building new ones.

The ideas here are my own, of course – but not totally. I see them everywhere. They leap up and live, too often unnoticed, unnoted, and unrecognized, in the valiant religious of this time who, full of the Spirit and on fire with life, bury the coals and fan the flame of a world yet unseen but sure to come. In them lies the embers of the spiritual life that not only make contemporary religious life really religious but the future possible as well.

1.

Foreword: Grounds for a New Beginning

It is at best a difficult time for religious communities. The glory days of large congregations, bulging novitiates, and growing institutions is long gone for most communities, but clearly remembered nevertheless. Some religious remain wistful about it all, wondering what happened to their lives. Other religious – newer members, whatever their ages, whose religious life depends on what they themselves build now rather than on what has been lost from another era – are tired of hearing about it. To them, that past is ancient history and has nothing to do with them and their spiritual development. Their mind is on the present – its goals, its gospel dimensions, its meaning for their own fulfillment as people. What they want is a vital present. They see little in the chronicle of renewal that has much to do with them and their spiritual life. Nothing, I think, could be further from the truth. Unless we understand the heritage of renewal, its ideals and its social circumstances as well as its theology and its social aberrations, we cannot possibly understand why we do what we do at the present time. Or what we must do next. We cannot consciously shape a contemporary spirituality as well as a humane lifestyle or an effective ministry if we do not know why we do what we do. Fashioning the present depends on our understanding it. Anything else will surely be, at best, good will gone awandering.

There are few instances of social change as pervasive, as encompassing or as redefining as the kind of restructuring that has taken place within the Roman Catholic Church in general and within Catholic religious orders in particular since 1965. The close of Vatican Council II ushered in the beginning of over 25 years of experimentation and social adaptation in age-old groups of both monastic and apostolic religious, particularly women, all of whom had been painfully out of sync for several hundred years. There is more than enough historical and academic data to provide reason to wonder if such a major restructuring of established institutions, any institution, is even possible. Sociology and social psychology are boneyards of celebrated institutions which failed to negotiate periods of social change. In addition to the organizational considerations, however, there is at least as much theological question now of whether religious life is viable, necessary, or desirable at all in this new world of the "lay vocation" and the newly emphasized "priesthood of the people." In a period of declining numbers, the question is a significant one. Are we seeing the demise of a once important but – in the face of a newly achieved educational level in the Catholic population at large – a now largely unnecessary labor force in the church?

The question alone is the measure of the depth of misunderstanding that surrounds the notion of the role of religious life. The fact is that religious life was never meant simply to be a labor force in the church; it was meant to be a searing presence, a paradigm of search, a mark of human soul and a catalyst to conscience in the society in which it emerged. No religious community ever set out to do everything that needed to be done for society in any given area. Religious simply did what was not being done so that others would see the need to do it too.

The confusion demonstrated by the question may arise from the fact that religious life, any form of religious life, ever came to be defined as anything other than an alternate form of Christian life discrete from either the married or single state simply by virtue of its communal dimensions. When, in the 11th century, Pope Urban II, a monastic, attempted to define the newly emerging group of Augustinian canons on the grounds of what they did rather than what they were in order to distinguish them from the only form of religious life that he knew, the notion of types, forms, and religious roles became a serious one for the future of the whole church. The problem may be that entirely too much emphasis has been put on the relationship of religious life to the mission of the church rather than to its relationship to the mystery of the church. The question has become, "What do religious do in society?" rather than "What must religious be in society?," and that twist of consciousness has made all the difference.

With so great attention given to the definitions of types and the distinctions between orders, commitment to religious life gradually became thought of more as a canonical form of life than a charismatic form of life, more as a set of rules to be followed than a set of ideals to be sought. It came to be treated more as service than as sign. Unfortunately, the implications of those very subtle but very real differences of perspective are cataclysmic. If our chief concern lies in the work that religious do, then when the work fades – for whatever reason – the life itself comes into question. If it is its canonical structures rather than its charismatic impulses that we look to for validation of its value, then when its organizational forms change, we may fail to recognize it. If it is the service it provides rather than the sign it gives that makes religious life valid, then when the service is accomplished the life runs the risk of becoming an anachronism.

Therein, perhaps, lies the explanation for the present situation in religious life. The revitalization of religious life does not lie in the redefinition of its forms; it lies in the rekindling of its sense of purpose, its claim to meaning in the face of new concerns and present realities, some of them institutional, some of them philosophical. The world that is changing around us changes us, too. We simply do not have the luxury to stand in place anymore. The important thing is that in our zeal to save the institution we do not destroy the life. The important thing is that we become what we are meant now to be in a world which, in the throes of a new beginning, is taking us with it.

Contemporary religious life has been deeply affected by four elements common to institutions as sociological entities everywhere at this moment in history. *Culture* has marked its form; *feminism* has concentrated its voice; *incorporation* in society has blurred its presence; and *enculturation* has sharpened its perceptions and made more diverse its expressions. As a result, religious life does not live outside the real world anymore, as it did even in its immediate past when it was fashioned more by medieval standards than contemporary theology. On the contrary, it is now immersed in the present to the point of potential obscurity unless and until it becomes more a spur than a shadow in today's society.

History is a kind ally to religious life but an albatross of immense proportions at the same time. A sense of history frees religious life from absolutizing its 19th-century forms. At the same time, its long history can also constrain religious life to enshrine a past grown quaint but useless. It is important to remember, then, that those same four social elements – culture, feminism, incorporation and enculturation – have long been sociological factors in the effectiveness and direction of religious life. The problem is that they have seldom been named and, too often, have been plasticized in time to the point where the value of religious life became the only question worthy of its highly effective past but seriously comatose present.

Religious life has declined at every major change point in history. At the same time, religious life has always revived at every major change point in history as well. The difficulty lies in choosing one of these possibilities rather than the other. At times of major social change, some people respond by clinging even harder to the past, some by ignoring it completely. This age of ours has been no different. For 25 years, religious congregations have dealt with both rigid conservatism and rash revolution. In our day, too, then, the issue becomes what dimensions of each of these areas are affecting religious life at the present time, what problems and prophetic possibilities do they offer to the present effectiveness of religious life, what human needs do they answer, what of each of them is leading to the decline of religious life and in what of each lie the seeds of the future.

The Relationship Between Culture and Religious Life

The relationship between culture and religious life is tightly woven. Across every period of history, religious life has been a source of social enlightenment, a center for education, a place of personal liberation as well as a place of spiritual growth. At one point in history, religious life was largely the preserve of intensely committed spiritual people who felt that the road to a better life lay in the negation of this one. In a later period, it developed into a harbor for pious widows. At another moment in time it provided a center for devout royalty until, by the 11th century in many places monastic life had become in essence the spiritual monopoly of the nobility, the only people who could afford the dowries necessary to support the communities. Still later than that, until far into the 20th century, however, religious life revived again, this time as centers of dedication for women from all social classes. Here women found the opportunity to give themselves to the questions of life and human development far beyond the scope that would be afforded them within the confines of marriage as it was then defined. Most women then, and even now in many parts of the world, realized that as women they would be confined to the margins of the male university system, if they were allowed in it at all, and excluded almost entirely from public positions and professions, from the pursuit of the great questions of life, from the pool of human thinkers that forged systems and defined laws. Religious life and religious life alone guaranteed a woman any real degree of internal autonomy and personal expression, limited as it was.

Clearly, religious life both reflected and responded to the social realities of the world around it and the development of the people in it, even in periods when it became most intent on shutting itself off from the concerns and agendas of the rest of society. More than simply a state of methodical spiritual search, religious life grew out of the soil around it. In some periods of history religious congregations energized the culture around them; in other periods it simply reflected the culture at its worst. But, the point to be remembered: it was never free of it.

Because religious life comes out of a culture to challenge it, it also embodies that culture in the mindsets and personalities of its members, in the agendas and questions of its times. When religious life fails to respond to these shifts in emphasis and content, religious life fails its culture and the culture rejects it. Religious life must be a conscious and creative response to the culture in which it exists or it is at best a pious pretense of the spiritual life, a therapeutic exercise in personal satisfaction.

Through its very immersion in the culture out of which it springs, religious life demonstrates the needs of the society around it, reflects its struggles, becomes a sign of judgment on its questions, or a sign of decadence by its distance from them. Religious figures, those who make the defining questions of humankind the centerpiece of their lives, have been recognized by every people of every culture, time, and place to be light in spiritual darkness, to be memory of life's ultimates.

It is important to realize, then, that one thing religious life is not is a perfect state of life for perfect people. It is not a state of life where perfection is even supposed. It is a state of life where effort is assumed and failure is taken for granted, where the human quest rather than the deluded notion of human flawlessness is the content of life. Only through consciousness of its frailty, the religious life of every peoples proclaims, may the human condition take hope. A monastic tale, for instance, reminds us of visitors from another age who were trying to determine for themselves the purpose of a monastery. "But what do you do in the monastery?," they asked the old monastic. And the elder replied, "Oh, we fall and we get up; we fall and we get up; we fall and we get up again." The religious pursuit, not religious perfection, is the proper subject matter of religious life.

Religious themselves mirror the struggles of the time by defining them, facing them, dealing with them in their own lives, not by running away from them as if spirituality had something to do with running away from the great questions of the age. Religious life, in other words, in its untiring efforts to assess, evaluate and give spiritual energy to the culture of the time, manifests to any people of any period of history those things in it that must be dealt with if the culture itself is to come to terms with its own demons, release its own gifts, develop its own wisdom.

It is not surprising, then, that in contemporary culture, religious life is a cauldron of the very issues that touch this society as a whole. The questions of independence, consumerism, individualism, community, self-gratification, sexuality, public morality and the spiritual life are key concepts in religious congregations today, just as they are in the society at large. A society that realizes the cultural dimension of religious life cannot assume as we did in the past that formulas, prescriptions, rules, horariums, superiors, and the repression of the human agenda are the spiritual answer to the social undercurrents of the age. On the contrary, to fail to develop the kind of spiritual life that is capable of facing these issues and working them through so that others, seeing some prevail in the struggle, may walk the same road with confidence, dabbles in religious adolescence rather than in adult spiritual development.

The choice between the decline and revival of religious communities at a time of major cultural change lies in the degree to which religious congregations recognize the missing values and major needs of a culture and raise them up for human reflection and response. The danger to renewal is that religious congregations will mirror the culture but fail to challenge it.

The revitalization of religious life does not lie in being different from the culture in which ground it grows; it lies in being keepers of the cultural values needed to save it. Revitalization does not lie in symbolic separation from the world; it lies in being genuine stewards of what is best in it. History is clear proof.

In the face of Roman patriarchy, Benedictinism flourished because it offered a new model of human community made up of slave and free, rich and poor, lay and clerical, all of whom were equals, had voice, served one another, sought spiritual depth rather than secular power. In an unsafe and warring world, Benedictines offered hospitality to everyone and provided order and stability to a world reeling from the fall of the anchor institutions of the Roman Empire. Francis of Assisi confronted the world with the first formal protest of obscene wealth by embracing voluntary poverty in solidarity with the poor. In the face of the fast-emerging and rapacious commercial order that would eventually reduce whole peoples to poverty while it enriched beyond conscience some few others, it was Francis who provided the first critique of it. In later centuries, newly formed apostolic congregations brought values of universal care and concern to a class-ridden and increasingly insensitive world. Compassion, insertion, and human potential were the cultural problems of the era immediately before our own, and liberty, equality, and fraternity the liberation cry of people who for centuries had been serfs and plebeians. The response of religious to a culture where classism choked the life out of people born bright but not born rich was to give them care equal to the best, give them education to make them competent, give them confidence to make them part of a society that did not care for them at all. And they succeeded. And they flourished. Not because of what they did but because of what they brought to society because of what they were – contemplative critics, passionate prophets to the ages in which they grew.

To whom has religious life been prophetic in cultures before this one? The answer is a parade of little people who, without the commitment of the religious of the day to another set of values than the ones that were the currency of the time, would have been ground up in systems before this one and left on the sideroads of civilization to fend for themselves: the illiterate, the abandoned, the dying, and the disenfranchised.

The challenge to contemporary spirituality, to the religious of our age, lies in the fact, then, that the great cultural questions of life have changed again. Education is a given now; health care is a national agenda; suffrage and fair labor standards legislation are things long since established. Now globalism, ecology, industrial slavery, peace, spiritual sterility, and sexism have become the issues of the age, the crux of human survival, the gauge point of every institution.

There is not a six-year-old alive who is not struggling with the questions of American culture, who is not being taught independence and immersed in consumerism and encouraged to be dedicated to the self and who has not been raised awash in self-indulgence and given to the narcissistic. Those things are what this culture is about. Those are the things, then, that religious life, too, must be about at this moment in history. Those are the things that must mark its aspirants and plague its sages. Those are the things that must shape its spiritual practices and guide its reflection and challenge its voice. It is to these things that religious must turn their attention if anyone in this culture is to find need of them at all. Religious must be part of the exploration of the times, not intellectual and devout refugees from it, not institutional bureaucrats or social service workers, or they run the risk of being a subculture without purpose, of existing for their own sake, of being spiritual runaways where they should have been inspiriting light, of embodying a religious life that no one wants at all.

It is a function of religious life to raise up the questions of the age to the conscience of the culture of the time so that culture has a spiritual companion, a spiritual spur along the way.

What is yet to be seen in our generation is whether or not the religious of this age are free enough of their present cultural heritage of privatism, individual development, individualism and personal religion to pursue a new set of values themselves. The old questions, the ones to which we responded so well – freedom of conscience, education, religious pluralism – are coin of the realm now. The qualities which we were told in the past would sanctify us – a military type of obedience, a kind of religious ghettoism, the excesses of self-abnegation – are not the virtues that will sanctify us now. On the contrary. Past value systems of achievement, security and national parochialism have resulted in peaks of economic domination, militarism, and national chauvinism that is bringing the West to a new kind of moral degeneration. What is needed now is a model of political compassion, universalism, an ecology of life, justice and peace if the planet is to survive and all its people are to live decent human lives. What is yet to be discovered is whether the religious of this time either hold these values themselves or will dedicate themselves to making them evident for others.

What religious life needs now is the cultivation of virtues, of spiritual disciplines that enable religious to respond to these new issues with personal strength, contemplative consciousness, and common focus.

Clearly there is a clinging to internal agendas in the name of religious perfection when real religious commitment must be radically public if the gospel to which we say we dedicate ourselves is to be real in our lives. The truth is that no one needs to have religious pursue the agendas of the past in the name of religious life. Not only are such pursuits irrelevant to the point of the absurd, they make a sham of the very question of holiness itself. Sanctity does not lie in the development of spiritual children, it lies in the cultivation of saints, of those people who take the world on its own terms and by seeking to bring the world closer to the reign of God, bring themselves closer in the process.

Feminism

Culture is not the only factor in the shaping and the significance of contemporary religious life, however. Feminism has found a new home there as well. It is not the first time that the role of women and women's issues have found an outlet here. Our foremothers may not have been "feminist" in the political sense of the word but they were without doubt women in search of their own humanity.

For over 1500 years communities of women have lived independently of male religious organizations, governed their own institutions, developed their own works, built, managed and financed their own enterprises. To discuss the rise of feminine consciousness without discussing the rise or decline of religious congregations of women is to lose a wealth of women's history, a plethora of women models and a treasury of women's accomplishments. Hagiography, folklore and the archives of religious congregations are full of the stories of strong-minded women who challenged bishops and bested them, confronted popes and chastised them, contested the norms of the society and corrected them. Most of all, women's religious life has been significant in the education of other women. Feminism, the consciousness of the graced and gracing nature of women despite the subordinating role definitions to which they were subject, is one of the gifts of religious life across time.

First, women went to the desert alone when women were not permitted to do anything alone. Then, women formed themselves into self-regulating groups when women had no legal rights in the society at all. Then, women took upon themselves the education and care of those for whom male society at large had no interest, no care or no disposition to provide public resources. They labored for the physical incorporation and the psychological worth of women in general. Like inch-worms across history, little by little, they brought women to an educational plane where the impact and import of women was finally discussible on grand scale.

The one thing women religious did not do for women as women in ages past has become the religious feminist's concern of the present time: They have identified themselves with the struggles of women everywhere, even in the church. They have become more conscious of feminine consciousness itself rather than simply being conscious of women. They have become aware of the systemic oppression of women and committed themselves to the structural transformation of society. They have allied themselves with the question of the spiritual wholeness of women in what is a male-controlled church. It is from within the institution itself, in other words, that women religious have brought to the scrutiny of that institution in newly feminist ways their age-old predisposition toward women.

This scrutiny has taken multiple forms, many of them public, many of them internal. It has become a very pressing question. The institutional church says in its official pronouncements, at least by implication, that it does not need scrutiny. Women say that in the light of an alternative reading of the gospels, it does. The situation is incendiary. It is also part of the current answer to the question of the prophetic dimension of religious life.

Religious communities of women have given institutional outlet to the movement for the use of universal language in liturgy and church documents, the modeling of women as preachers of the Word and the question of women's ordination. What may be even more important, women's communities have, for all intents and purposes, in many instances become spirituality centers for Christian feminists from all denominations. The impact of all of these activities lies less in the activities they generate than it does in the doubts they raise, both inside and outside of the institution.

At one level, their involvement in the women's movement has raised concern among women religious about the real value of women to the church, despite lifetimes of service and authorized commitment. At another level, the protest of women religious concerning the role of women in the church affects the organizational structure of the church itself. In some cases, the women's movement has brought strain to women's communities themselves between those who see the questions as dangerous to the faith and those who do not. Finally, involvement in the women's movement has led to critical evaluation of the effects that nuns have had on other women in the church. What did women religious themselves teach about male-female roles and what was its influence on other women?

That, then, is the difference between the woman-centeredness of past eras of women's religious congregations and the feminism of this one. For the first time, as a group, women religious have begun to question the very theology upon which past models of womanhood have been based. Women religious themselves are having to question their own role in the subjection of other women. Women religious are beginning to examine their own present actions in their attempts to refuse to participate in the perpetuation of an internally inconsistent system that preaches one definition of the equality of women but structures another.

It is a delicate sociological moment. On the one side lies the rupturing of an ancient and valuable institution in the church, on the other side the authentic evolution of the human community along the lines of its highest spiritual aspirations, its deepest Gospel values, its truest theological insights. To choose for values which model a lower level of humanity is to betray the best religious traditions of the past and, in the face of a generation looking for the fullness of creation, it is to risk at the same time the possibility of giving future to a women's institution that does not bring courage to the women's question itself and may even obstruct it.

The Question of Liminality, Boundaries, Immersion and Identity

Culture and feminism are only two of the major issues shaping religious life today, however. The third issue, seldom discussed at this point of institutional development but always close to the surface of the religious agenda, is the question of liminality, boundaries, immersion and identity. The identity issue in contemporary religious life is without doubt at one of its most critical and profound levels in church history. For centuries religious commitment implied a degree of disinterest in the affairs of the world in which they lived. Dualism, the war between the spiritual and material dimensions of life, cast suspicion over anything not directly related to the spiritual life. Jansenism, the theological rationale for making withdrawal itself the spiritual hallmark of the religious lifestyle, rooted religious life in a rigid lifestyle far outside the flow of new life patterns in an urban, industrial society. By the 19th century, the deed was done: Religious life had become a culture within a culture.

The separation of a subculture from a society is a relatively simple process: titles, badges, uniforms and walls have all served the purpose for a variety of groups far beyond the confines of Roman Catholic religious congregations. The structures give mystique, give mystery, give glue to a group. They do not, on the other hand, necessarily signal the social import of the group. It is possible to be different in society without being important to it. It is possible to be a group segregated within a group in highly visible ways and still arouse wonder in the dominant body about the value of the group. The questions of its purpose and significance, both theological and social, begin to be answered in more and more symbolic ways.

On the other hand, a group without an identity is no group at all. The basic sociological principle that people join groups in order to do together what cannot be done alone becomes especially pertinent where religious are concerned. Religious life, after all, is "a total institution." Women and men give their very selves to it whole and entire, day in and day out, all the days of their lives with nothing else to strive for, no place else to call home, no one else with whom to share their lives. The question is: Why? The answer is: In order to be in the world the kind of contemplative presence that manifests, that requires the reign of God, to be some part of bringing the world to the kind of creation that God wants it to be. The identity of the group, in other words, is social and institutional as well as personal. The group itself must have a reason to exist, an identity within a society, a boundary between itself and others that is permeable but prophetic.

In the United States, two things have happened which make the identity question more important to answer and more difficult to answer at the same time. First, the personal identity of religious has been blurred. Not only do individuals not wear uniforms, a factor which once, unfortunately, made the identity question unnecessary to address at all, but the question of identity is tied up in two even larger issues – the Catholic identity *in toto* and the American identity itself.

What used to be the Catholic presence in the United States – strings of institutions which created a Catholic ghetto and set out to transcend it at the same time – fell victim to rising costs, a declining number of vocations and a changing attitude in the Catholic mind itself. The fact is that the religious/Catholic identity crisis did not occur because Catholicism had failed in the United States. On the contrary, Catholic identity became a problem precisely because it had succeeded. The goal of preserving the faith and inserting the Catholic population into a pluralistic society had been achieved with resounding success. So effective had the church and its religious institutions been, in fact, that the Catholic population no longer considered it essential – or in some cases, even desirable – to be seen as part of a Catholic subculture. Slowly but surely they began to leave the Catholic enclaves which had sheltered and sequestered them from public harm, to insert themselves with confidence into the wider population, to go to public hospitals and to send their children to public colleges. Slowly and steadily they blended into the culture around them in almost everything except churchgoing. To be Catholic became a religion rather than a way of life.

Confirmed by the teachings of Vatican II, faced with the practical problems of the costs and distance and more limited offerings of Catholic institutions, authorized by the nondenominational character of U.S. life in general, a new kind of Catholic laity emerged, more culturally mingled than ethnically obvious, more publicly acceptable, more cosmopolitan in choice and character. The incarnation of the Roman Catholic Church in the United States, the enculturation of the U.S. Catholic, the end of the ghetto church, had begun.

Some religious, formed in the evolving society, moved with the people out of the schools into broader Christian horizons. Others stayed in Catholic institutions and were faced head-on with the dilemma of attempting to maintain a Catholic identity in the American identity. They found that they could provide shelter for the elderly poor, for instance, but only if they met the specifications prescribed for such programs by the U.S. government. They could go on educating the poor but only if they met the curricular, technical and professional requirements demanded of every other educational institution certified by the government. They could work with refugees but only if they met the citizenship criteria laid down in Washington for foreign residents. They could do migrant day care programs but only as long as the facilities they provided satisfied the norms set down by federal officials. They could give health care but only if they maintained the standards and procedures provided in public institutions. And, if they were women, they could work in parishes but only as long as they saw themselves as subservient to the male priest pastor to whom canon law ascribed the real authority and responsibility for the work. In the end, after more than a century of well-defined roles, institutional identity, and official recognition in the Catholic subculture, religious became invisible functionaries. The very nature of a Catholic institution itself became clouded.

Confronted with the social implications of a pluralistic culture and face to face with the larger identity questions of feminism, religious life and church, religious began to see that they were no longer needed as a work force in the church. They were needed to be what they were meant to be all along: a spiritual voice, a countercultural sign, a prophetic presence in the culture. The question was for what and how? If anything became clear, it was that religious were definitely not needed now where they had been needed before the great ethnic shift of Catholics into mainstream culture. What was not at all clear anymore was the question of Catholic character and religious mission. Enculturation itself became a paramount issue in religious life.

Enculturation

The conscious sculpting of a life within life that had become the unquestioned nature of the religious vocation by the mid-twentieth century was, perhaps, the most obvious characteristic of religious commitment to be brought into question by the new ecclesiology of Vatican II. For the first time in modern history, the church no longer defined itself as the Kingdom of God under siege. Now the Church was "leaven" and by implication, therefore, so was religious life with it. The theology of transcendence gave way bit by bit to a theology of transformation. Enculturation, the need for outsiders to plunge themselves into the minds and souls and hearts of the people with whom they now live, became a conversion point for religious life itself. It was time to bring the spiritual life back into the real world.

One of the more complex elements of the present struggle to find the place of religious life in contemporary society, if any at all, however, lies in the fact that just as Catholic identity itself had shifted by the time of Vatican II, so had the identity of the nation and its people. To be from the United States in 1950 meant to have a messianic responsibility to maintain U.S. culture and to export it abroad so that the rest of the world could come to the same standards of life and quality of political character that Americans knew. There was a great atheistic enemy against which to defend Christianity, a battered Europe to rebuild, a Third World to convert and save for democratic – read: Western – capitalism. What went unnoticed, apparently, was that the white-faced, starched-shirt world that had won a world war was not the world that could win the peace. Things had changed.

The United States became a hotbed of scandals – political, financial and military. The Third World debt, centered in North American banking institutions, the threat to the planet from U.S. nuclearism and toxic waste, a growing population of poor in the wealthiest nation in the world – the United States itself, wars waged against countries made of thatch, the repression of popular liberation movements in Central America and escalating violence in U.S. cities, left the nation in disarray. Its values were splintered, its self-image confused, its quality of life seriously damaged. Religious who had given their lives to educate the generations that now profited from the spoils of the system began to rethink their own values, their own motives, their own educations.

If there was ever a moment in modern history that proved the sincerity of religious orders, the response of U.S. religious to the changing conditions in the country itself marked the continuing inspiration of age-old charisms over the institutional interests and personal comforts that had accompanied the success of Catholic projects past. Religious moved in dizzying numbers out of the schools in the suburbs that their ancestors had made possible and moved into soup kitchens and peace centers and parish work and political advocacy roles in the center of decaying cities. But not all and not totally.

With one foot in each generation, religious have made the cosmetic changes of clothing and lifestyle that democratize their position in the population but may have yet to make the changes in emphasis and presence that would make them apparent in it. They have changed the way they live, but they have not necessarily made plain, even to themselves perhaps, the social purpose for doing it, the fundamental moral reason for doing it, the theological mandate for doing it. Many "permit" members to begin new ministries for the sake of the person's interest. Whether or not they encourage such ministries for the sake of the poor and the integrity of their charisms is too often another question. For instance, few orders as orders are really identified with the major questions of the age – nuclear disarmament, women's issues, ecology or systemic poverty – as once they were unabashedly identified with Catholic education, Catholic immigrants and Catholic health care. Many orders have a few members in each area who do prophetic work, but today only some congregations, as groups, take public action on today's specific issues as they once did at great cost for the education of unwanted immigrants or the care and cure of the abandoned.

Enculturation for its own sake, however, can only diminish a group that finds itself so much like everyone else in the society that they are just like everyone else in the society, with no clear purpose, with no obvious reason to exist. Enculturation is the process of taking on the characteristics of a culture in order to add something of value to it, not to be consumed by it. When religion is properly encultured in a society, it finds meaning in the environment and provides spiritual significance to the experiences of the people there without having to import and overlay forms on them that are foreign, that never fit, that obscure the present for the sake of some ideal past someplace else. On the contrary, enculturation is the process of recognizing the sacred in the familiar. It is not meant to be a process of losing oneself in the banal.

The danger of undirected enculturation is that religious life will become too vapid to be necessary to anyone. Enculturation is more than a matter of wearing the same clothes and working at the same places and having the same standard of living as everyone else in the area, regardless how measured each of those accumulations may be. Enculturation is the responsibility to celebrate the real blessings and take on the real burdens of a place in order to become converted by them ourselves and thereby to make them more apparent, more bearable for others. It is a concerted effort made with conscious choice not for the sake of personal comfort but for the sake of the reign of God.

It is necessary to a culture that those who value it and understand it, devote themselves to maintaining its lights. It is the function of religious life to concentrate on fanning to flame the spiritual lights within them that enable a people to go on treading the path to wholeness. It is not that only religious do it or even that they do it better than other Christians. It is instead the fact that religious must, by virtue of their very definition of themselves, do it always, do it publicly and do it consistently from the vantage point of the poorest of the poor on whom the gospel concentrates.

The question then of the value of religious life in contemporary society can only be answered by examining the qualities contemporary religious mirror to modern society in light of the challenges of the culture within which they exist, the model of the feminine that is demonstrated there, the prophetic nature of their works and the quality of their presence in society. What religious emphasize in their own lives at the present period of history has implications for religious life for generations to come.

Religious in the United States, like religious of every culture and era before them, have had a great deal to do with shaping U.S. culture as we know it and in modeling it as well. Achievement, conformity and productivity have been the hallmarks of their history and so the watershed of their present dilemma. What the world needs now is a sense of the universal, not the parochial; a vision of world community, not national or religious chauvinism; a new economic order, not institutional aggrandizement; an unremitting unmasking of the kind of systemic sin that is designed to make the rich rich and keep the poor poor, not a paltry sense of moral pettiness that insulates a people from the world around them; a contemplative sense of the will of God for the world, not a plethora of personal devotions. What the culture needs right now is a religious life that is broader than the culture in which it exists; a religious life that is more than religious theater; a religious life that brings the glaring light of conscience to a world grown coarse under the weight of an amoral, if not immoral, kind of capitalism.

The poor of the world and the very planet itself need a religious life that brings brave voice to good deeds.

Groups that purport to be religious but take no courageous stake in the women's movement relinquish the gospel for the cult. It is a declaration of feminism to follow the Jesus who raised women from the dead, commissioned them to proclaim his message, taught them his vision, raised them in dignity, recognized them in public, became human himself through the sacrifice of a woman, and let women follow him in public. To fail to do the same ourselves is to make a mockery of the messianic message of liberation for all. To educate women but provide no equal social space for them where their education can have social meaning; to cure women but to leave them without the fullness of human possibility; to teach that women are fully human and then to deny them full spiritual adulthood is to mock the theology of the incarnation, baptism, grace and redemption itself. Without a commitment to feminism, the church itself cannot be credible in this age. Public consecration, once itself a prophetic posture, is no longer enough. Religious orders must demonstrate this commitment to the development of women in ways that are real: in structures that are equal, in liturgy that is inclusive, in a lifestyle that is independent, and in ministries that not simply serve the oppressed but resist the oppression.

Oppressed, rejected and misdefined women need religious women and men to bring recognition to their own. The price to be paid for responding to women will be a high one in this church and this society. The cost to be borne by the church if we do not respond to the needs of women with courage and authenticity and vision will be even higher.

To be effective in this culture, religious life must have genuine identity. Religious must be seen as more than vowed celibates, more than a productive labor force. Religious must make their celibate identities count. They must make their contemplative identities real.

The function of celibacy is not to be loveless; the function of celibacy is to love without limitation, to lay down my life in loving commitment to more than those who love me. The celibate can afford to be courageous. The celibate can afford to be rejected. The celibate can afford to be outside the systems and the servitude that hold others hostage to their responsibility for the survival of others beyond themselves.

Contemplation is the core of religious identity, the energy of the religious life. The central truth of religious commitment is that it is about more than dedicated social work. Steadfast social workers have been part of every culture in the world from Nazi Germany to segregated South Africa. They bind the wounds and meet the pleas of any people too weak to provide for themselves. They do it out of a sense of human compassion and social order. Contemplatives, on the other hand, are driven by a sense of the unremitting will of God. No social order, however well it works, however much it is accepted by the population at large, is enough to quiet their restless passion for universal life and unboundaried possibility. The contemplative stands in the middle of society with the eye of a cosmic dreamer and announces the dream.

A wounded and abandoned world needs religious lovers who love everyone with the heart full of Divine madness.

Enculturation is a great religious gift. It is enculturation that pronounces good everything that is. It desacralizes nothing. It touches everything that is with dignity. It dedicates everything in the world to Divine purpose. It makes incarnation real. On the other hand, enculturation can simply serve to trivialize what should otherwise be momentous. It can level and homogenize all of life to the point of the commonplace. Wedding ceremonies done to rap music, prayer sessions done with coffee cups in hand, religious life lived in college dormitory style without purpose, without depth – all run the risk of diminishing the sense of the sacred in life or of obliterating the distinction between the meaningful and the meaningless within us.

The forgotten of the world need religious who live their humanity, like them in everything but despair and dedicated to bringing hope, bringing help so that life tomorrow can be better than life today in the name of the One who came "that they may have life and have it more abundantly."

The poor, the planet, the women and men who seek to release a feminist vision of life in a world gone calculatingly insane with machoism, those dry in soul and loveless, the oppressed and the forgotten – all need the comforting presence, the concerted voice of religious who have learned that a truly spiritual life is not an exercise in spiritual massage, it is the goad of the gospel.

It is not that religious life is necessarily more "religious" than any other state of life. It is simply that it must be, first and foremost, devoted, bound and responsible for raising the spiritual to the level of the obvious, for calling the attention of the world to the spiritual dimension of its actions. It must covenant with the world at large, it must promise, it must guarantee to watchdog, to monitor, to announce the questions, the concerns and the spiritual context of the major agendas of the world for the sake of the spiritual search in the rest of humankind.

The real question, obviously, is not the inherent relation of religious life to the world. The question is whether or not the religious of this time are psychologically and spiritually able to make the new relationship real. The real question is whether there is enough energy left in congregations and enough life commitment left in their members to direct their focus now not as individuals in the process of self-development but as groups in the pursuit of social impact.

To respond to this culture, they will have to be willing to critique its present values and to model new ones.

To make a difference in the lives of women, they will have to give space and substance to the women's issues of this time in both church and society and they will have to demand it of themselves as well.

To reestablish their identity in contemporary society they will have to bring contemplative presence and a prophet's courage to everything they do.

To enculturate successfully rather than simply to become like the culture around them, they will have to stand for something larger than themselves and they must come to stand for it once again as visible, high-risk groups. They must, in other words, give real presence to present questions in real ways.

What values and virtues are needed if religious life in our time is to be as holy, as impacting, as real as the religious life before us that saved civilization, spread the faith and inserted the poor and marginated into societies that did not want them, would not deal with them and often exploited them?

Catherine de Hueck Doherty wrote once, "I would not have liked to live without ever having disturbed anyone." The question is not, "Should religious life exist?" The question today is, "Is religious life disturbing enough in our time to meet the great need that the world has for it?"

The real question is whether or not there is still enough fire in these ashes to bring to flame the energy that is needed now to make religious life authentic. The real question is, what qualities are necessary now to bring religious life back to the white heat of the Gospel life? What, if anything, is virtuous, is holy about religious life as we know it today? What, if anything, is there in religious life today that makes it safe and secure for tomorrow?

The fact is that the new virtues of religious life are clear and compelling. The challenge is simply to embrace them, to articulate them, to rely on them to do for this day what virtues of a different hue did for the past. The challenge is to release in ourselves the strength of soul it will take to do for this time what we did for the last, to unleash on a society gone sour with a pathological centeredness on the self and on a globe gone wild, the call of God to community.

The purpose of religious life is not survival; it is prophecy. The role of religious life is to bring to visibility what is Good News for our time now, not to preserve a past long gone and no longer germane to the challenge of new questions. The role of religious life is to make sacred the present. The question is not, "Is religious life really religious life anymore?" The question is, "What are the spiritual disciplines of this age, as valiant as those before them but tempered to the time?" What of all the present qualities of religious life, in other words, makes for the kind of spirituality that can fit contemporary religious life for the 21st century?

2.

The Fire in These Ashes

Almost 30 years after the close of Vatican II, the ecumenical council called by Pope John XXIII to initiate reform and renewal in the Roman Catholic Church, another Pope, John Paul II, convened a Synod on Religious Life. The purpose of the Synod, the Vatican announced, was to assess the changes initiated by the Council, to evaluate the present condition of religious life and to give it new direction. The effects of the Vatican Council were widespread and revolutionary. Change erupted everywhere; excitement flared everywhere; new directions were legion. The Synod on Religious Life, on the other hand, happened without fanfare and went quietly away, no new initiatives generated, apparently, no great hopes raised. Nothing really new or energizing came out of it at all, except perhaps a consciousness of the consciousness of the church about religious life.

In my more rational moments I know that possibly the best thing that can be said for any Synod – and this one on religious life most of all, perhaps – is that it did not obstruct what it cannot create and must not destroy. The final document notwithstanding, at least the synod itself did not raise a hue and cry about the present state of religious life, which is far better off in its heady lurching toward new life than most people realize or many people admit. The fact is that all the Synods in the world will not, may not, and cannot renew religious life, however official their renderings. Only religious can renew religious life.

In simple terms, religious life is not simply a resolution to be ratified. All the official meetings in the world cannot, by dint of discussion or legislation, make religious life religious. Religious life is far more than any legislation on the topic. Religious life is a gift given to the church to make the gospel life present across time in bold and tangible ways. It is a grace let loose in a temple of cement, a firestorm on a winter horizon. It is more spirit than law, less law than the energy for the God-life that pulses through a group making it impervious to obstacles of a lesser level, however real, however reasonable they may be.

Nevertheless, whatever the historical truth of its development, the church has always domesticated religious life – something like saddling a fractious pony – but no amount of canon law has ever really been able to break its irrepressible spirit. Over and over again religious life has broken out of its traces to reach for the unreachable, despite the fact that it was at the same time reaching for the ecclesiastically illegal. Religious life created Christian communities in the midst of social chaos, preserved culture in the throes of barbarism, ministered to women left illiterate by the male systems around them, honored the sick and dying and useless levels of society, gathered up the orphans, attended to the underlings, spoke for the unspeakables of the land and ventured far beyond the pale of every nation to reach out healing hands to other people in other places. And this period of religious life is no different in this regard from equally difficult periods before this one.

Religious of this age have abandoned their medieval uniforms to become leavening parts of a hurting world, stepped over taboos to walk the way with the divorced and homosexual and unchurched, left the tried and true but

initially radical institutions that had finally become establishment to start new ones that were again only barely toler-
ated – soup kitchens, and hospitality houses for battered
women and hospices for the homeless and peace and justice
centers in a world where violence was being theologized.
Religious life has always been a messy, untidy thing in the
heart of the church and never more so than now. "The prophetic dimension" of the church, some of the documents call
it, "a charism," others say. Whatever the words, the concept
is an important one: A charism is a gift to be recognized and
set free, not an organization to be controlled. All the canons
in Christendom cannot fabricate out of legalisms what does
not already exist in the spirit. A charism is mercury, not clay;
spirit, not office; a movement, not a labor force.

Synods, on the other hand, by definition, are part of the
apparatus that sets out to define and to direct what, in this
case, may at its best need to resist definition and flee direction
like the plague if religious life in the labor of death is to live
at all.

One thing the Synod on Religious Life did do, however,
is to unmask both the tensions and the strengths of the time
so that we can appreciate all of them for the gifts they are.
The Synod became a kind of tug of war between the keepers
of the institution and its official innovators, religious themselves. It is, as a consequence, almost amusing to follow its
work. What each feared in the other may well be each group's
fundamental gift to the church – keeping the institution stable
and moving it on at the same time. In that case, the real
problem could well occur only if either side finally wins the
field for itself.

Responses to the *Instrumenta Laboris*, the working paper
of the Synod, reflected very clearly the elements of force and
counterforce at play in religious life and church today. The
hierarchy talked control; the religious pointed up the freedom needed to go on being newly prophetic in a rapidly

changing world. The hierarchy referred to canonical categories and rules; religious insisted on autonomy and spontaneity.
The hierarchy referred to the vows; religious concentrated
on the development of a particular kind of lifestyle. The
hierarchy stressed obedience; the religious emphasized the
need for affirmation and encouragement to continue their
daft and daring following of a Christ who cured lepers on the
Sabbath. No doubt about it, negotiating this Synod was like
walking through a minefield with snowshoes on. And for that
reason alone, if for nothing else, everyone who ran the course
for us is certainly to be congratulated. And thanked.

Problem with the Synod on Religious Life

No, the problem with the Synod on Religious Life, I think,
does not lie in the fact that there was one. The problem lies
in two much more subtle concepts: In the first place, the
Synod talked about charism, but was much more immersed
in caution than it was in the heady energy of the Christ-life
gone wild in our time. It was clearly more an exercise in
church than it was an excursion into the Spirit. It obviously
set out more to control the Spirit than it did to confirm the
kind of selfless risk and simple openness of the Vatican Council that inspired it. As a result, the Synod lost the chance to
turn the tide of ecclesiastical suspicion about the twists and
turns in contemporary life into a chorus of hope and confirmation. Instead, it hung like an old leather strap over the
heads of the participants. It breathed no life, set no fires,
generated no heat, stirred no ash. All it did was to make
tentative forays over old territory with new politeness. It gave
the distinct impression, in fact, that the whole exercise was a
bad imitation of an old nighttime scene: parents frowning at
the bedroom door while children lay, barely breathing and
pretending to be asleep, on comic books they were forbidden
to read. But no one is fooled. The parents know that some-

thing new is going on and want to correct it if they can only figure out what it is, while the children play innocent but unconverted in their determination to take new steps in life. The problem is that neither one of them announces that they are dealing with people mature enough now to turn out the light for themselves when they're ready, and who will turn out the light when it suits them, and who must turn out the light for themselves, if they are ever to be genuinely adult. Instead, the parents keep playing parents and the children keep pretending to be children, both of them knowing secretly that they are not.

The point is that we cannot talk about religious life as the prophetic dimension of the church in one set of papers and then treat it with painstaking caution and parental distrust in all the others. On the contrary, this is an exercise of equals with two different roles in the church who must engage with one another in order to take both the church and religious life to the next stage of development.

But there is another problem with the Synod, as well, which ranks as more taboo, less often admitted even than the first concern. The Synod was based on the assumption that religious life is still a viable, a necessary, a healthy, a good, an inspiriting way of life, still capable of sanctification, still bent on universal beneficence. But no one ever asked the question. So no one ever answered it. That means, of course, that no one ever really asked what religious life was good for now. And no one ever asked what religious life really needed now if it is to have energy and give energy, have vision and give vision, have courage and give courage. No, all the Synod did was to dust off the tried-and-true, the steady and predictable, the clear and the certain, the institutional and the theological. It did not face the new questions; it did not raise a new round of applause for those religious who are one more time in history taking the church where the church might otherwise never go. Instead, it opted to deal more with insti-

tutional values than with the charismatic dimensions of religious life it talked about and, in the doing, did little to unleash
the charismatic at all.

It is not a new situation in history, this use of form and
law and tradition and system, to answer questions of the soul,
but I would have wished for a different approach, the one
described in *The Sayings of the Desert Monastics*. "Once upon a
time," the story goes, "Abba Lot went to see Abba Joseph and
said, 'Abba, as much as I am able I practice a small rule, all
the little fasts, some prayer and meditation, and remain quiet,
and as much as possible I keep my thoughts clean. What else
should I do?' Then the old monastic stood up and stretched
out his hands toward heaven, and his fingers became like ten
torches of flame. And he said, "Why not be completely turned
into fire?"'

What religious life needs right now, perhaps, is to be
turned completely into fire again. Then, none of the tensions
will matter and all of the tensions will only make each of us
more of what we were meant to be in the first place.

3.

The Keeping of the Coals

For the last 30 or more years, ever since the very advent of Vatican II, the lifestyle of religious congregations and their role in society have been analyzed to the point of paralysis. For the religious involved, this chancy, exciting, wearying, ambiguous period has become the greatest asceticism of all, harder than hairshirts, more demanding than conformity, more difficult than rituals and disciplines. "Time," Tennessee Williams' character Tom comments in the *Glass Menagerie*, "is the longest distance between two places." For religious who thought that the renewal of religious life would be a task, not a lifestyle, that has without doubt become a hard truth. It has been years of change, decades of adjustment, whole lifetimes of uncertainty, ambiguity, conflict and confusions.

For those coming to religious life now, the task is to rebuild religious life for decades to come out of the flimsiest of traditions perhaps, but for the generation that came to religious life before or during Vatican II, the task was to dismantle a system heavy with the accretions of the ages. Suddenly, after years of cloistered routine and immutable custom, religious life became a kind of social experiment, an exercise in organizational tinkering and social insertion. The renewal of religious life took on all the character of an archeological dig. Layer after layer of its theology, its history,

its institutional forms, its organizational impulses, its psychological effects were laid bare one after another in order to
expose for general view its workings, its impulses, its social,
emotional, and personal ramifications. Every element, every
assumption, every custom, every jot and tittle of the rule, no
matter how longstanding and sacrosanct, became refreshingly
suspect, tiringly suspect. Here was a social scouring of immense proportions, one of the most total in social history,
perhaps.

While anthropologists who claimed professional interest
in subcultures sat, for the most part, idly by, an entire way of
life turned on its axis a full 360 degrees. Cataclysmic in proportion, but almost invisible in its long-term effects, change
became the norm for groups who had changed almost not at
all, some of them, for hundreds of years. The academic exercise of renewal took on a life of its own. It became for many,
in fact, the *raison d'être* of community life itself. The purpose
of religious life became to renew religious life. And all the
while that happened institutionally, individual religious became more and more alienated from the life itself. Renewal
simply did not stem the outgoing tide of membership. Many
left to marry or to devote themselves to professions where the
service continued unabated and the stress of life in cultural
transition did not pervade. Few entered. Those who stayed
found themselves staying for far different reasons and greatly
different goals, many of them blurred at best, than the ones
that had brought them to religious life in the first place.

Now the question became whether or not anything at all
would remain of a lifestyle once generally considered permanently unchangeable, commonly considered superior. Worse,
the real concern became whether or not there was any compelling reason for religious life to exist at all. What could a
religious do, for instance, that any layperson could not now
do as well? What was the purpose of celibacy, the virtue of
poverty, the value of an obedience that could be as psycho-

logically deleterious as it was organizationally efficient? Why would a person live in groups of strangers with little but faith for comfort, even given all the changes for the better where human values – personal development and social quality – were concerned? If it was not a "higher" vocation, a guaranteed passage to eternal life, a place of social privilege and public respect, a measure of goodness and a moment of innocence crystallized, why do it? In fact, do what?

Past and future became the time warps of religious life. What had brought it to this point and where it was going consumed the organizational agenda of group after group. The present took on the character of a crucible between what had been and what was coming. At the same time, for individuals in every community, for those for whom the organizational agenda took on the flesh and blood of everyday life, the present ceased to have much of a character, a value, a respectable quality of its own. What had been and what would be, not what was actually going on in each of us spiritually, through us spiritually, consumed us all. Yet, all the time, dailiness felt more and more sterile, more and more unimportant, more and more uninspired, except perhaps as a kind of holding place over life. Life became a scientific study of a permanently faded past or a series of strategies geared at shaping the future. Everything counted in the spiritual hopper but the now, everything was grist for the spiritual mill but the now. Now was lost time, waiting time, hard time. One kind of religious life had gone and another kind of religious life, everybody promised, was coming. Someday. Few, if any, said anything about the nature, value, energy and life quality of religious life now. The present itself, it seemed, had little value, little character, little quality, little of the spiritual life.

Clearly, the question of whether or not religious life has made a valuable contribution to church and society in the past is passé. History gives clear confirmation of that. The role religious orders and congregations have played in the development and preservation of art, learning, architecture, social development and church life in ages past reaches the levels of the incalculable. Indeed, we stand on valiant shoulders. Foundresses and founders battled for their vision, even against the church, until church and state alike called them blessed. Congregations built empires of social service agencies. Individual members in every congregation rose to civic prominence in generation after generation. Clearly, to question the past value of religious life is, at this stage, almost boring.

Surely, too, the consuming question for religious life in our day must be more than what shape religious life shall take in years to come. Frankly, who cares? That we must live and think in such a way that we make the future possible is one thing. That we should abandon a consciousness of the energizing quality of the present in order to live in the far-off-but-not-here is entirely another. To prepare for the future is one thing; to forfeit or forget or forego the power and purpose of the present is entirely another. What religious need to know at this period in history is whether or not religious life has any value now, is good now, is worth living now, is holy-making now, is beautiful now.

The question of present value is a much more difficult one than whether the past was good and the future is possible. The question is whether or not there is purpose in the present. And if so, what is its purpose? Can religious life be revived? Should religious life be revived? Is there any fire left in these ashes?

Grieshog

The Irish have a word for it. *Grieshog,* Gaelic speakers tell us, is the process of burying warm coals in ashes at night in order to preserve the fire for the cold morning to come. Instead of cleaning out the cold hearth, people preserved yesterday's glowing coals under beds of ash overnight in order to have fast-starting new fire the next day. The process is an extremely important one. Otherwise, if the coals go out, a whole new fire must be built and lit when morning comes, an exercise that takes precious time and slows the more important work of the new day. The primary concern, then, was that the fire from yesterday not be permitted to burn out completely at the end of the day. On the contrary, coals hidden from sight under heaps of ash through the long, dark night were tended carefully so that the fire could leap to life again at first light. The old fire did not die; it kept its heat in order to be prepared to light the new one.

It is a holy process, this preservation of purpose, of energy, of warmth and light in darkness. What we call death and end and loss in our lives, as one thing turns into another, may, in these terms, be better understood as *greishog*, as the preservation of the coals, as refusing to go cold. Our responsibility, both new and older members of us, may simply be to stay religious till the day we die so that religious life may live long after we do.

"Time is the substance from which I am made," José Luis Borges writes. "Time is a river which carries me along, but I am the river; it is a tiger that devours me, but I am the tiger; it is a fire that consumes me, but I am the fire." (Labyrinths: *A New Refutation of Time*, 1964) I am, in other words, what is to become. What is going on around me is going on within me now and will or will not happen because of me. I am both the vehicle and the substance of the future. What I am now, religious life will be in the future. There is no future without me because the future is within me.

The thought sobers a person to the center of the soul. Religious life will not die in the future unless it is dead in religious already. Each and every religious alive today is its carrier. Each of us is its life. I myself am whatever good it is. When people ask about the state of religious life, they are asking about me. What will religious life look like in the future? The answer is an easy one. To get a glimpse of the coming religious life, all a religious has to do is to look in a reflecting pool: Is there energy of heart shining out of the eyes there? Is there a pounding commitment to a wild and unruly gospel there? Is the spiritual life aglow there? Is there risk there? Is there unflagging commitment, undying intensity, unequivocal determination to be what I say I am? Or has the old glow gone dull? Is life now simply a matter of enduring the days and going through the motions? Or is religious life in a brand new arc demanding more discipline from me and giving more life through me than ever?

Too Much Surrender

If religious life suffers from anything in the present, it may well be from too much surrender to demise and too little realization of what it means to maintain the coals, to fan a fire. Resignation reigns now where recklessness should be.

The notion that religious life is dead has become commonplace. For too many, perhaps, it has also become an operational motto, a given, one of the facts of a life gone sour in mid-stream. The temptation then is to make our highest aspiration simply the intention to live life out rather than to live it to the fullest with all the certainty and depth that we lived it in the form before this one. And what about the women and men – newer members of religious communities, few, yes, but stalwart nevertheless – who come looking for spiritual fire among us and are getting damped by the weight of the self-fulfilling prophecies of pending demise? What is the responsibility of the fire-tenders to those who come to a fire but find that the fire has been allowed to go cold? Is the problem that there are fewer vocations or that there are fewer fires blazing high enough to yet be seen?

The truth is that the problem of change pales in the face of the problem of anomie. If religious life fails, it will not be because religious life changed. It will be because the religious of this period of history have lost a sense of the spirituality of the present and sold their souls instead either to the past or to the future. If religious life fails, it will be because we ourselves, our individual and corporate selves, lost a sense of the value of the present, the power of the present, the challenge of the present, the meaning of the present, the sanctity of the present.

Scripture, on the other hand, gives us a model that is quite the opposite. Jacob first works seven years for Leah, the bride he did not seek, and then, still driven by his original vision of life, works seven more for Rachel, the bride he sought in the first place but whose giving was delayed. In each case, Jacob works just as hard, with just as much fervor, with just as much care. In each case, the work is just as important. In each case, Jacob never stints, never quits, never withdraws his heart though each case is different. Jacob, clearly, is the patron saint of contemporary religious life.

Jacob teaches us continuance of spirit in a time of change. Jacob teaches us that reversals of our life-plans are not nearly the obstacles to life we think they are. Through Jacob we come to see that we are not always capable of recognizing the value of where we find ourselves in life. In Jacob we realize that reversals simply attune the heart to higher things again and make us listen for the original voice, for the first sound that moved our souls, for that moment of innocence when everything fell away between the soul and God and made life a dance over glass instead of an endurance test. If anything, Jacob teaches us most of all that it is not change that threatens religious life; it is stinting that desiccates the soul; it is stinting that wrings life out of life; it is stinting that turns us to hollow and shrivels us to dust. Holding back on the promise is worse than breaking it. Once the fire goes out, once the coals go cold, once the stoking of the soul begins to stop, it is not the cold that kills, it is the inability to rekindle the flame that once we held within the breast and now have left to smother that damps the heart and confuses the mind, wearies the body and slays the soul.

But it is not a dying time for religious life. It is an important time for religious life, a time of great new birth in embryo, a time for total surrender and total involvement at the same time. This generation of religious will decide the birth of the next, aborted or stillborn, bright-minded or open-souled.

It is what is happening now in religious life that will measure its goodness, its holy tenacity, its depth of spirit for ages to come. And what is happening now is the task of a holy tenacity and indomitable zeal that enables the young to expect the impossible and the old to be willing to begin again.

A Confusion of Spirit

The real tragedy of the present state of religious life, then, is not that it is in turmoil. The real tragedy is that it suffers from a confusion of spirit. When religious life, we thought, looked most alive – when religious robotization had reached the peak of the industrial model that spawned it, producing products at a great rate and organizing people by the thousands – it was actually most dead. And did not know it. Questions had stopped; thinking had stopped; even personal spiritual development had been reduced to modes and exercises and formulas. The regular life had been substituted for the spiritual life.

At the same time, now, when religious life calmly and commonly declares itself dead, it may be more alive than it has been for generations. For the first time in decades, perhaps in centuries, religious life pulses with new energy and stands steeped in the greatest questions of the time. Surely it

is the religious of the church, the ones who claim a consuming
passion for God who will question first the questions that the
world waits to fathom: Where is God in a world that flirts with
magic and is inoculated against mystery by the seductions of
science itself? What links the material to the spiritual and
makes the spiritual material at the same time? What makes
for church? What defies the oppressive claims of gender?
What determines age? What defines death? What measures
life? What is authenticity and what is not? What makes for the
spiritual purposefulness of a period without apparent purpose? What is religious life itself and what spirituality under-
lies it at a time when the questions are crucial but the coals
are low and the ashes are growing cold?

The spirituality of religious life today is neither the spirituality of the cross nor the spirituality of the resurrection. The
spirituality of our time is the spirituality of Holy Saturday: a
spirituality of confusion and consternation, of ineffectiveness
and powerlessness, of faith in darkness and the power of hope.
It is a spirituality that carries on when carrying on seems most
futile.

This is not a time for quitting simply because the past is
past and the present is unclear. This is not a time for not
beginning just because the journey is uncharted. In fact, what
an older generation of religious promised a lifetime ago may
only now be beginning to come to pass, to make its demands,
to reveal its meaning. What a newer, younger generation of
religious do now to create the next moment in religious
history out of the dust of the old may only come to promise
in years to come. But that's all right. The commitment basic
to religious life has little or nothing to do with what religious
do. Religious commitment is about why they do what they do.

The spirituality of productivity is over. Religious do not
give their lives away because an institution runs hospitals, no
matter how good those hospitals may be. They do not limit
their own life options simply to multiply prayers for those

whose life activities never end. They do not exist to provide a labor force for people who, if they did not have this one, would never notice. In a society where the once radical concerns of education, medical care and social services have gone mainstream, specific works cannot justify, explain or impel religious life. What must drive religious life today is the spirituality of creation, where, for far too many, hope dies in darkness and smolders in ashes waiting for the dawn of that day when simply the right to ask the difficult questions themselves will be understood as an act of faith, a sign of fidelity to the God who calls to us from the other side of mystery.

Scripture defines a clear model of service and change, of change and new service where commitment alone bridges the gap between old certainties and new challenge. In Genesis, Jacob sets out to achieve one thing and finds himself faced with a new and different task. Jacob laid his life down for Rachel, and got Leah instead. It was not simply a private blow, a life challenge, a moment of struggle for Jacob. It was also, in the divine scheme of things, an act of personal faith that sowed the seeds of a whole new world for the Chosen People at large. In this day, too, older religious know well the meaning of a life that begins in one thing but becomes another, and younger religious know what it is to have the burden of beginning again in the spirit of the first. What is important is that the relation between the two life tasks never be forgotten, never be misunderstood. Jacob made a promise and kept it through both its dimensions.

When Jacob was given the right to marry Rachel, the dream of his life, he also got contention and challenge far beyond his wildest notions of them. He got a second life.

Contemporary religious life has lived two lives, as well. The first was staid and standard, a good life with clear rules and certain rewards, a private exercise of personal virtues. The second life, on the other hand, is wild and unclear, makes demands on us we never dreamed possible, demands that everyone, young and old, begin again and, most of all, has a meaning far beyond the church alone, the Catholic ghetto, and the struggle for personal salvation. This time religious life has meaning for the world at large.

Like Jacob laboring for Leah, it is time for us to begin again, this time to achieve the purpose we came for in the first place. The French proverb teaches, "Everything passes, everything perishes, everything palls." To have something leave us is not a sign of loss. It is only a sign that we are meant to go on to something else, to what, like Jacob, we set out to achieve from the very beginning.

But that will take a keeping of the coals.

4.

On the Way to a High Mountain

Someplace along the line, for a number of good reasons perhaps, it has become unfashionable to say that the one and only purpose of religious life is the single-minded search for God. Better answers – ministry, public witness, community needs – have been devised to satisfy the rationalism of a secular and technological world. None of them seem to survive the heat of the day. Good works, moral concerns and right-minded human interactions are the responsibility of the entire Christian community, not simply of professional religious types. To use those concepts alone to understand the meaning of religious life, then, smacks at least of the aberrant, if not the bogus. The idea of social concern is simply not enough to justify the reshaping of common life patterns by a whole population of people. Whole institutions are devoted to doing good works, most of them organized by lay people; almost all of them nonsectarian. Religious need not apply. By those terms, there is no need, no basis for religious life at all.

On the other hand, Mother Sylvester, my first prioress, made two trips to our novitiate yearly. In both of them, she came to ask us only one question. Patience was her hallmark; she tutored us with measured steps. In fact, she viewed with great benignity the fact that most novices failed the test rather routinely at the time of her first visit. At the same time, she was anything but complacent if we failed it at the time of her second one. "Why have you come to religious life?" she asked each of us in turn, arms folded under her scapular, head tilted down to scrutinize us over her glasses as she scanned us around the table. At first blush, we made up wonderful answers: "To give our lives to the church," the pious said; "To save our souls," the cautious said; "To convert the world," the zealots said. But no, no, no, she signaled with a shake of the head. Not that. Not that. Not that. "You come to religious life, dear sisters," she said sadly, "only to seek God."

Only to seek God. The answer stuns in its simplicity. In its ubiquitousness. In its universality. In its demands. The awful truth of the answer changes everything. For the person who cannot find God here, staying here is a mistake. For the person who does not seek God here, leaving here is an imperative. For the person who can find God better someplace else, leaving here is a grace.

It was a simple answer but, whatever the era, it endured. More importantly, it sustained. When religious life was rigid to the point of being silly, "seeking God" sustained. When hours of work and equal hours of choral prayer numbed the body to the point of insensibility, "seeking God" sustained. When the loss of human contact and human comforts stripped life of most of its mortal joys or healthy outlets, "seeking God" sustained. The fact is that the answer, simple as it may be, uncompromising as it is, cannot be improved upon, even today. Today most of all, perhaps. This generation above all, a generation in which all the foundations once considered immutable have shifted, ought to know the truth of that like few others ever have. When absolutes fail us and ministries falter and even the church, perhaps, becomes a distant and discomfiting place for those with new ideas or disturbing questions, the idea of seeking God and God alone takes on new power in life.

For this generation of religious, in the course of whose lives an entire system has crumbled around them, there has seldom been less of a refuge than the idea that the unfolding mystery of God is the only reason worth our going on through a lifetime of darkness to even more darkness yet to come. When the whole world cries out to us, laughing, "Enjoy!" or "Why?" or, worse, "Ridiculous," when there are no sure answers to the constant predictions of institutional death and the macabre kind of resignation that comes with apparent and invariable failure, it is then that unclarity becomes insight. The truth is that there never was any good reason whatsoever to enter religious life other than "to seek God."

The Universal Human Quest

Seeking God is the universal human quest. It is common to all cultures. It is the fundamental human project. It is the common denominator of all the human enterprises. It is common to all human beings, necessary to all human endeavor, central to all human effort and ultimate to all human activity. What is more, it is the only reason that makes any sense whatsoever out of religious life. Religious life is not just another way of life. It is a way of life intentionally organized to pursue the human quest for God.

For the religious, immersion in God becomes the single, unmitigated and unnuanced reason for making every other plausible, worthy and determining motive in life – love, money, children, personal success – secondary to the life pursuit of Mystery among us. Immersion in God is the concept that brooks no other greater than itself. It is the question that undergirds every day, the longing for which any kind of loss, any amount of change, any degree of effort is acceptable.

We have too often, however, been seduced with greater intensity by other explanations for religious life, all of them valuable and all of them true to a certain degree. We have sought to be "relevant." We have set out to be "incarnational." We have given ourselves untiringly to "the option for the poor." We have devoted ourselves to "the transformation of structures." We have evangelized and renewed and revised and reformed until we dropped from exhaustion. And all of those commitments are good and necessary, holy and worthy of attention, fundamental and imperative. But through it all, one thing and one thing only can sustain religious life, can nourish religious life, can justify religious life: The religious must be the person who first and foremost, always and forever, in whatever circumstance, seeks God and God alone, sees God and God alone in all of this confusion, in all of this uncertainty and, whatever the situation, speaks God – and God alone.

If religious life is to save a fire and fan a flame for whatever kind of religious life to come, the emphasis must then shift again. We must move from concentrating solely on what religious do to why they do it and what religious are to be. God-seekers, religious are to stand like beacons in the night so that others, too, may remember and never forget the only real reason to do anything in life, the final measure of everything we do. Religious must give as much conscious attention to the things of God as they do to the tiny, private, personal little worlds of the world in which we all live, however challenging, good and necessary those personal spaces may be. Otherwise, religious life is just one more social institution to be succeeded by social institutions after it, rather than centers of contemplation where, we can hope, the mind of God can touch the mind of humanity.

For over 25 years now religious have concentrated far too much, perhaps, on congregational charisms and canonical types as the bedrock of renewal. It is possible, even, that we have paid a great deal too much attention to being

"Benedictines" and "Mercys" and "Franciscans" and "Ursulines" – to being some particular group with a particular history to maintain – rather than to being centers of reflection where the gospel and the globe are brought together for all to see. We have certainly given more attention to being renewed congregations than we have to being evangelical groups, contemplative people, centers of reflection, and harbors for those broken in heart or homeless of soul. We have certainly spent too much concentration on being church people, canonically correct and ecclesiastically defined, than we have on being Jesus people. We have risked giving too much attention to defining charisms than to bringing them alive again in our own time in us.

And therein lies the problem. We have been talking about one kind of thing when all the time, down-deep, we knew we were required to rivet ourselves on another, to be what we really entered religious life to be, to participate in the great spiritual quest in the modern world, without which no life is worth anything at all, and to speak it without ceasing.

It is not what we do that makes us religious. It is why we do it and how we do it that sounds the bell of authenticity throughout a rightly suspect world. What the world does not need surely is one more group of people, however well-intentioned, who proceed without clear priorities, without operational principles that distinguish one good activity from another, without as much concern for justice as for the kind of charity that maintains oppressive systems rather than reforming them, without genuine openness to the poor of God for the sake of God. It is seeking God and the reign of God that makes religious activity really religious. Anything else is good-hearted but ill-defined, kind but not religious, well-meaning but not really effective, polite maybe but not prophetic. Being steeped in the mind of God is the essential religious activity. Everything else simply follows from that.

When Abraham left the country of Ur, it was in the very going that he found God, yes, but more than that, it was God for whom he went. Because Abraham was attuned to the voice of God, he survived what would have been impossible for him to withstand otherwise. Abraham's journey fails over and over; the path twists and turns over and over; the circumstances threaten over and over; authorities obstruct him over and over, he loses resources over and over. But Abraham feels no defeat in any of them, not in the failures or the changes or the disapproval or the turns in the road. Because he has talked to God, because God has talked to him, only the voice of God itself is the measure of his meaning and his success.

Keeping the Voice of God Alive

If the fire is to be kept for another generation, religious life in this time must be about keeping the voice of God alive no matter what happens to the works of the congregation or the structures of the order or even the ecclesial definitions of the life.

But we cannot fool ourselves. The spiritual quest is a spiritual quest. Talking about it does not do it. When we take no time to immerse ourselves in the gospel because of the gospel work we do, we have made ourselves our god and our work our end. And it will fail, if not outside of us then inside of us for sure. Religious who do not attend to the spiritual life do not have one, no matter how good the motivation, no matter how cultivated the professionalism, no matter how laudable the works in which they are engaged. Without a commitment to the spiritual life, we bury no coals for the future, light no fires, leave no embers for kindling the ongoing quest in others to come.

What is to be discovered, of course, is whether or not the two elements of the human condition – the material and the spiritual – are really portion and parcel of one and the

same life. Is life able to be lived intensely only when it is
intensely compartmentalized? Are seeking God and seeking
life at the same time diametrically opposed? The institutional
legalisms, of course, insist this is the case. For years the church
has pitted one element against the other – especially for
women – in a dualism that turned even the spiritual life into
a hierarchy of types. Some people went to what the canons
called "the active life" and said prayers; others went to enclosed communities and, contemplating God, forgot the
things of creation. The ecclesial message was clear: The active
life, involved as it was in the lives and needs of people, in
"material" rather than "spiritual" things, was the less total,
less heroic route to God. Apostolic religious life, such a cos-
mology concluded, was therefore not quite as high a state of
holiness as the enclosed life – as if walking through the world
God made was itself a threat to the spiritual life. The cloistered
life, on the other hand, with its separation from "the world"
was the stuff of high virtue – and heavenly approval as well,
we were led to believe – as if striving to live cut off from
creation made life holy. It was an unfortunate distinction. It
was also, I believe, a false one, the damaging results of which
are only now beginning to be apparent in religious life, whatever its ilk.

We talk about "active" life and "contemplative" life as if
those were true opposites and concepts in tension. The fact
is, however, that it is the "active life" and the "cloistered life"
that are opposing categories. Contemplation is basic to both.
The terms "cloister" and "contemplation," in other words, are
not synonyms. Contemplation, the coming to see as God sees,
is required of us all. For some people, cloister is a vehicle to
contemplation; for others, God is found in the faces of the
poor. In both cases, contemplation is both the beginning and
the end of the enterprise.

Having divided the spiritual world into "active" religious
and "contemplative" ones, however, instead of identifying

them simply as non-cloistered or cloistered, we have over-looked the very nature and life of Jesus. Or are we saying that Jesus, walking the dusty roads of Galilee, healing dirty people, smothered by beggars, exhausted from the pressure of the crowds, the questions of the pharisees, the needs of the children, the cries of the poor was not a contemplative, was not immersed in God, did not see God in everything, did not see the world as God sees the world? Wherever did we go so wrong in our understanding of the spiritual life, and what does it mean for religious life now?

The spiritual quest, the search for God in time, the upbuilding of the reign of God, the attention to God where God is present in people drives religious life and impels it careening through all the other goals of life, no matter how praiseworthy those other goals may be. The spiritual quest tolerates no compromise with any aspiration less than the felt presence of God in this place, to these people, in this venture.

The spiritual quest in us is what always demands more than life has to offer. The person whose life is bound up in the spiritual quest never knows failure and never expects success, never knows success and never gives in to failure. It is finding God in what we do that is the measure of our success; it is walking with God wherever we go that makes failure impossible.

To be totally committed to the spiritual quest means to respond over and over again to whatever beckons us beyond where we are to something even closer to the mind of God for us. The spiritual quest takes a person away from this ministry, away from these people, away from this place over and over again in life, so that God can break in to us and to the world in fresh and vibrant ways. When where we are has become enough for us, the spiritual quest has died in us. The spiritual quest means that we will never be satisfied with anything less than the spiritual life lived to the hilt in the life-growing graces of the material life around us. The spiritual quest does not flee life. The spiritual quest seeks God in everything, everywhere and will not cease until each step of the quest comes to holy completion. Where God is, the spiritual quest demands that we go there. Where God is not, the spiritual quest demands that we bring to the situation the vision of what the moment lacks. To do those things, however, we must ourselves be steeped in the spirit of God, be alive in the spirit, be attuned more to the spirit than to the task.

Sign of Trouble

The first sign that something has gone wrong with religious life, then, is when work, any work, becomes more important than the quest itself and what it demands of us here and now. The work of teaching, the work of healing, the work of pastoring, even the work of being a religious itself is not as important as the seeking. Wherever we are, whatever we do, we must do it with the greater will of God in mind. That is, of course, the difference between being a religious and being a social worker. The social worker does a work that must be done and is worth doing. The religious falls so completely into the arms of Christ, the mind of God, that nothing will suffice except to become what one seeks: the merciful One, the loving One, the truth-telling One, the One who says, "Go you and do likewise." Point: it is not a particular work that captivates the religious, however good it is, however much it is needed. It is the God whom she holds in her heart and finds in prayer, in people, and in the transubstantiation of the planet into the reign of God that impels her life.

To seek God, then, is to be impelled to action. Separating the search for God from doing God's work creates the very antithesis of the spiritual quest. The trick, of course, is to maintain the delicate balance between the two. In this century, religious life has suffered from both extremes. Religious dualism, taken to its outside limits, says one of two things –

on the one hand, that prayer is enough and on the other hand that work is enough. The generation in which we find ourselves has said both. We have made public work the basis for evangelization and the defining characteristic of religious life. Having had those fail or falter, we have called religious life itself a failure as a result. We have also assumed that the cloistered life was closer to heaven because it was more distant from the world around it. Neither posture can be further from the truth if the prophets were really of God, if Jesus was really a contemplative. History confirms the fact that it is in the integration of the two – of action and contemplation, of contemplation with action – that religious life thrives. Our greatest contemplatives have been our most active people: Hildegard and Bernard and Teresa of Avila. Our most active people have been our most contemplative: Catherine of Siena, Charles de Foucauld, Ignatius Loyola. In our own time, the monk Thomas Merton did not operate a peace and justice center but he did make the question of peace and justice a burning question for the church. At the same time, the Jesuit priest and his married brother, Dan and Phil Berrigan, did operate a peace and justice center, but only out of an intensely public spiritual perspective.

Clearly, what religious life needs now is the cultivation of the sacred, not separate from the secular, but out of its very substance. The function of religious life is to keep the question of God – and God's questions – high on the horizons of the world so that, from whatever point, they may be seen and pursued by everyone and anyone. Without a strong, clear, witnessing spiritual life absorbed in the mind of Christ and grounded in the gospel, the best work in the world is purely social work, whether it's done by members of religious orders or not. Then the spiritual questions, the basic questions, fade from world view, then life itself becomes barren and questionable, then the ashes chill and there is nothing left to give a coming generation that is really worth keeping.

The task of religious life is not a task at all, it is the application of the great questions of life to all of life's dimensions. The religious does not do charity without asking, "Why this injustice?" The religious does not teach without asking, "What must be learned that will change the world?" The real religious does not attempt to act before contemplating the reason for it, the consequences of it, the costs of it and the contribution of it to the coming of the reign of God. The religious life makes contemplation a very active thing.

The purpose of religious life is the pursuit of the spiritual quest, the preservation of the spiritual questions, the articulation of the spiritual challenges from age to age, in whatever form and whatever season. But in that case, the current concern about the value of religious life is at least misguided, if not totally misunderstood. Is there any purpose left to religious life now that it no longer has as its hallmark the once great institutions raised to answer the major social questions of past generations? Indeed, and never more so. Now religious life has a chance to begin again, plumbing the gospels and shouting the questions with which they confront a coming world. The question challenging society now is not "Is religious life valuable?" As long as the Gospel is valuable, religious life will be valuable. No, the real question is simply, is religious life viable? Is religious life itself religious enough to throw itself upon the Gospels again, rather than upon the institutions which, though once they demonstrated it best, in this new age are now more mainstream, more *of* the culture than prophet *to* it.

But first of all, we ourselves must plumb the gospels. Every day. Always. Without flagging. In every situation. We must live spiritual lives that flame for all to see, yes, but most of all we must live spiritual lives so deep, so regular, so clear that we cannot be surprised by opposition. We must create in ourselves spiritual reservoirs that take us past every barrier in church and state with peace in our hearts and calm in our lives, knowing without doubt that the questions we ask are not of our making only.

Once upon a time, the Zen masters say, an old woman made a pilgrimage to a far away mountain shrine in the worst part of the rainy season. Stopping at an inn along the way, she asked for a night's lodging before beginning her climb up the holy mountain. "You'll never climb the slippery clay of that mountain in this weather," the inn-keeper said. "It's impossible." "Oh, that will be very simple," the old woman said. "You see, sir, my heart has been there for years. It is now only a matter of taking my body there."

There is no religious life without a genuinely religious life. But with it, everything else – the ambiguity of this period, the transitions of this period, the new social challenges of this period, the fire-saving purpose of this period – will be very simple.

5.

A Time for Risk

"Old age," Bette Davis said once, "ain't no place for sissies." Old age takes a special kind of courage. It depends for its energy on that rare kind of strength that goes on doing what must be done, not because it is easy, not because it is exciting but simply because it is worth doing. Old age, with its capacity for the long haul and its strength of experience, reflects a particular kind of quality, an uncommon gift for life. Old age is not the end of life, it is a stage of life that presents new challenges and calls for new kinds of responses. Old age brings its own gifts, its own responsibilities. Most important of all for religious life at the present period, though, may be the realization that old age touches every human thing, not just people.

If religious congregations, themselves far beyond the first blush of adolescence, need to learn anything at all at this time in history, the special character of old age may well be it. There is a great deal of life in old age. It simply depends on how we live it. We can die years before our time or we can live until we die. Every living thing finds itself faced with the choice.

Religious life, then, is dealing with old age on two levels. First, the age of the membership is rising. Even new members are usually older members now. Secondly, the age of the institution itself, with everything that implies in terms of community customs and cultural assumptions and habits of life and theological ideals, has shifted. The challenges, then, are equally clear. Older members must stay in touch with new ideas. Newer members must preserve their young-heartedness and fresh vision in an environment where the immediate past history may have for far too long been mistaken for eternal truth. Where age predominates, the community mind must become a young vision rooted in old values, or we may well confuse what we've always done with what we're supposed to do.

This period of religious life, then, having peaked in a past era and faced with building a new one, cannot tolerate the kind of resignation that precedes death. To be a truly spiritual life now, it demands courage of rare caliber.

Someplace along the line, everyone and everything gets older. The conventional wisdom in a culture where youth is a national anthem requires that at a certain age people give up the ghost to the next generation and go into a kind of dotage that waits with patience and passivity for death. It is no surprise, then, that in that kind of environment, people die in the doing of it long before their life is over. The process is a sad one. For those who die before their time, the past gets immortalized and even the thought of a future, life-giving and fresh, becomes impossible to imagine. Only what has been counts; what can be, must be, stands ignored. Without realizing it and for no reason at all, these doers of the living death become dull and doddering and boring people. Indeed, they can get very boring very young.

As a result, in this culture the very idea of age itself poses one of the greatest dangers to American religious life. Age becomes the intersection between American culture and American religious life. Here culture and the spiritual life clash, very subtly but very clearly. The conflict between what the culture thinks about age and what religious think about age requires resolution.

A youth culture sets points at which life, for all practical purposes and in multiple dimensions, ends. We end formal education programs and know that we have begun our professional decline. We reach the age of 40 and lose a sense of professional possibility. We retire from a position and lose a sense of public value. In such a social climate, religious life provides a counterpoint of qualities that point consistently to the immortal without thought of either end points or confines.

The culture "retires" people, shunts them out of the marketplace at earlier and earlier ages to preserve a fragile economy and adjust to a steadily increasing computerization. In the process, people who were once the movers and shakers of their small worlds become disoriented, feel valueless, see themselves as useless at the very age at which they may finally be experienced enough to know something. For many people in a society geared to productivity and measured by money, life ends just as it begins. Marked "old" now, life becomes a matter of going through the motions but going nowhere.

Religious Life Never Retires

Religious life, on the other hand, channels every minute of a person's energy and vision toward a point beyond life itself and so never really arrives, never completes itself, never retires. For the religious, life is always beginning, never actually finishes, moves always toward the next new moment of becoming. For the religious death comes, of course, but it does not come before every minute of life has been lived to the fullest. The death of a religious is not timed by the workplace or the social system nor is it attached to a particular age. There is always something important to begin at every stage of life, something new to learn, something important to give.

The challenge to religious life at this point of history, then, is to prove the implications of both attitudes toward time. To one way of thinking, time diminishes us and we quit long before we end. To the other way of thinking, time is simply a series of steps to fullness of life and so we never quit. The culture touts the fragility of age, religious life recognizes its pervasive power and purpose.

It is not true that age restricts us from living a full and vibrant life. On the other hand, it is true that age refines us and hones us and makes us new again. Age is precisely that point in life at which values change and virtue is renegotiated, when what we once thought was really important, really good is finally open to question, open to a new quality of choice. It is really only when age comes that we all decide freely not only whether we are really going to live or not but how we are going to live and why.

For the young and inexperienced, prudence often takes higher priority than risk. The young person who wants to get ahead learns early that the road is trod by playing the system, by conforming, by going along quietly, by threatening nothing and no one. Young people get the message very quickly that the better part of valor is to gain ground by treading carefully until experience compensates for lack of skill. As a result, young people, unsure of every step, are often inclined to cling to the ones they know. A conservative generation, we call them, when what may be closer to the truth is that every younger generation is under great pressure to be an accommodating one, give or take a few rebels here or there. Young people, too, in other words, have their own struggles with risk, all images of the wild and the reckless notwithstanding. Young people learn to wait patiently for their time to come.

For the old, on the other hand, for whom hard-won security may too easily become a temptation and success too smugly a given, caution may cement life in place at the very moment it most needs to be freed. Then the ability to risk, not the willingness to wait, becomes the ultimate measure of character and worth, of quality and happiness. That's why old pioneer figures are more a shock, more an influence on society than younger ones. Albert Schweitzer, Albert Einstein, Dr. Seuss, Mother Jones, Grandma Moses, Maria Balanchine stir the blood and kindle hope in us far more than the youthful types around them who, we know, may or may not stay the course, may or may not become what they set out to be, may or may not bring quality as well as fever to the fray. In fact, what can possibly be more dangerous to the status quo than experienced, fearless, confident older people who cannot be intimidated, cannot be controlled, cannot be punished for being obscenely alive.

The real truth is that new members who come to religious life looking for social security in a place that purports to follow the Jesus who was hounded by the synagogue, feared by the state, thought crazy by his relatives, rejected by his neighbors and loved only by the outcasts of society come to exactly the wrong place. The real truth is that old age is not the time to settle down at all. Not here. Not now. Not anywhere. Old age is the time to try new things with abandon and imagination if life tomorrow is to be anything but a long, sad rehearsal of yesterdays far gone. To live until we die may, in the final analysis, be the ultimate goal in life.

But religious life as we have known it is itself now old. Religious congregations are long past the burst of energy that comes with dedication to new projects and great endeavors and public triumphs. Religious life itself has passed a mile-marker of great import. The old work barely exists, is almost invisible, hardly counts in the plethora of similar institutions around it, most of them larger, wealthier, broader in scope than what had been the glory of congregation after congregation. Whatever the reasons, they are largely gone. So, the question plagues: Is religious life gone, too? And if not, what is the spirituality of this time? What can possibly redeem the sense of failure and disintegration that comes with seeing a period die the death of time before we are ready to let it go.

Life and Liveliness

What religious life needs now clearly, at a stage of abatement, is not resignation to death. It needs life and liveliness. It needs new purpose. It needs the faith to take new roads with new fervor and little fear. After all, what is there to lose when everything that was is lost already? At the very moment when the world would expect decline, require decline, religious life must refuse to be less than itself. Religious life requires risk now more than caution, more than conformity, more than the kind of conservatism intent on preserving the things of the past rather than the wisdom of the past. Religious life needs older members who refuse to give in to oldness of life and younger members who refuse to give in to oldness of soul.

To be in an old institution is no excuse for not thinking young ideas and doing young things. Rather, the very age of the institution demands it. To be old ourselves is no excuse for being dead, no excuse for being safe, no excuse for being sedate to the point of the comatose, no excuse for sitting back and waiting to be saved from ourselves. "Who shall deliver me from the body of this death?" the psalmist asks. And God's deafening silence is the answer. Only we ourselves can save ourselves from the death within us, old or young.

The fact of the matter is that it is not our obligation to preserve religious life. Our only obligation is to go to the grave being religious ourselves. We must stop looking for reasons, accepting excuses, telling ourselves the self-fulfilling prophecies that enable us to run in place. We talk about declining numbers and rising median ages as if numbers and time were the meaning of our commitment, the measure of our success. We talk about tradition and "the spiritual life" as if daily schedules and changeless rituals were the mark of our fidelity, the manifestation of our faith. We compare past forms to present forms and then find the new unacceptable, not because it is unfaithful to the spirit of the life but because it is unfamiliar. We talk about new needs and then find them impossible because of "the old sisters," not because they can't meet them but because we don't want to take the burden of doing them ourselves. We falter at the very point when, after a lifetime of prayer, we should be most strong and fail to become precisely what we have prayed to be all our lives: people of faith, people of prophesy. Instead, like everyone else in the culture, we count our institutions as signs of our success, our loss of them as symbols of our failure, as reasons to settle down and let the rest of the world go by.

Most painful of all, perhaps, is the possibility that the spiritual quest itself, once it has been shrunk to the level of schedules and routine, may itself become a trap. The "spiritual quest," in fact, can as easily become the death knell of religious life as any activism that springs from frenetic and unfounded change or develops out of social fads. The spiritual quest, most of all, can become nothing but a pious excuse for doing nothing spiritual at all. In the name of the spiritual life we go to bed early and ignore the poor; we get up early to pray and forget the exhausted; we live in our warm convents and forget the people in the tenements; we tell ourselves that we are too old, too young, too small, too insignificant to do the things we used to do and so we give ourselves permission to cease to be a presence, a prophetic voice. And we call it religious life. And we wonder why it's dying.

The problem with age is that it brings with it such a temptation to die before its time, to go into a kind of living death where every effort is too much and every energy is saved simply to draw the next dull breath. Some people simply curl up years before the onset of agedness and give themselves over to aging. They wait for death, die the death of lifelessness, go listless into a long gray night until, sure enough, death hovers around them like birds above a wounded animal. We see it all around us. Those who cease to live begin to die and those who go on living make death an anachronism. What we fail to realize is that communities can do the same. And often do. And have done. And are doing.

Part of the struggle of the time, of course, is that what was once young and required to be staid is now old but required to be spruce. Where religious life is concerned, of course, the problem may be that it was such a youth culture for so long that people forgot how to live after the age of 50. The war years' vocations set the stage for huge novitiates and early withdrawals. There were always younger people to carry the burden of maintaining the works so that people barely older than themselves could settle into a countrified routine of "religious life," no great burdens to worry about, no challenges to face, no visions to create. Just prayers to say and a schedule to keep and a routine to maintain once you were over 50. And all in the name of religious life.

It's a very sad state of affairs. Now, the number of really young vocations is slim. In this culture few people make any serious, long-term commitments at all – marriage, parenthood, career choice – until their 30s. As a result, almost everyone in religious life today is over 50 or nearing it soon. Not that there's anything wrong with being 50. Fifty is a glorious age: full of experience, full of wisdom, full of fearlessness. No, the only thing wrong with being 50 is acting as if life is over once we are. What used to be "old" in religious life is now young. In society, those who used to be considered old in society are now faced with beginning whole new kinds of life at that age, "retired" from life with years to live yet. It is a lesson for religious communities to weigh seriously.

Living Till It Dies

It is the virtue of living till it dies that is required of religious life now if the fire is ever to flame up again. It is the virtue of risk that religious life again requires: Risk in older members who thought that the great risks of their lives were over. Risk in newer members who were ingenuous enough to think that a life of established prayer and service is a life without risk at all.

Risk has some very tangible characteristics, however, many of them lost in a language gone soft from mindless repetition. The first thing to remember about risk is that risk is not a virtue unless there is a high possibility of failure. Risk, in other words, does not really exist until it requires something of us that seems at first sight, at least, to be almost certainly doomed to ruin but absolutely essential to begin. The trapeze artist who lets go of one swing in mid-air to snatch wildly at another one takes a risk. The philanthropist who takes a fortune out of the money-market to finance a private reha-bilitation project for delinquent children takes a risk. The reporter who spends hundreds of hours of unpaid time to expose political fraud takes a risk. The theologians who admit that they differ with the magisterium in matters of debate take a risk in the interests of intellectual integrity. But they are not alone. Risk is of the essence of the integrated spiritual life. The prophets who scorned the gods of Baal and de-nounced the king and scolded the priests and irritated the people knew what risk was all about. The widow Judith who went against an army with nothing but a maid-servant embod-ied the virtue of risk for all to see. Mother McAuley, Angela Merici, Mary Ward, Benedicta Riepp, all the great founders and foundresses of religious congregations took great risks because gospel risk was of the essence of the time.

Risk is not brazen talk by a warm fire on a dark night. No, risk requires insecurity. Risk demands the bold bet on the desirable but unsure thing. Risk is faith unbounded by reason.

Risk walks with God as its only sure companion. The religious congregation that risks its reputation for the sake of new questions and its benefactors for the sake of peace and its clerical support for the sake of women and its lifestyle for the sake of the ecological stewardship of the planet and its retirement monies for the sake of the poor walks the way of holy risk. It is not an easy way for religious life to go but there is no other way if the life is to be real, if the fire is to be rekindled from the flame of its past.

Risk energizes, enervates, drives adrenaline through the bloodstream of a group, makes life worth living again. Risk, ironically, makes life, life again. A religious congregation in a state of risk balances on the edge of life in a state of giddy fidelity to the past that brought them here in the first place. They become worthy of their ancestors and a model to the daughters of their old age.

Abandoning Renewal

The problem may be that we have for far too long been attempting to take risk out of religious life. We started renewal and then left it in mid-flight. We know that renewal has "slowed down." We do not realize that we abandoned it. We want the church to change the rules regarding the participation of women in liturgy and decision-making positions but we live within all the rules in the meantime, docile and dutiful, and risk very little to get it, not our reputations, not our clerical connections, not even the peace at our dinner tables. We want the ministries of the congregation to continue, we tell ourselves, but too often we concentrate more on funding our retirement programs than on subsidizing the ministries that are needed and trusting our retirement programs to take care of themselves if we take care of others, as our foundresses did before us. We vote in chapter after chapter endorsing postures, positions and actions that are wildly prophetic and prophetically wild, and then we retire to our separate little worlds and wait for someone else to do them on the grounds that we ourselves are too old, too unprepared, too tired, too involved elsewhere in more important things to shift direction now. Or worse, we support nothing at all that would in any way damage the reputation or the security of the group because "What good will it do to irritate people?," or so that we can "challenge without confronting." We want the future without having to pay the price to get it. We regard the local prophets with great suspicion and sink deeper and deeper into ourselves everyday. We become old religious sissies, far from the quality of the visionaries who withstood social, political and theological resistance of their time so that we would do the same in ours.

It is clear, then, that dull groups engender people dulled to life, blunted to the call of life within them and unresponsive to the call for life around them. All the retirement funds in the world will not save such a group. All the "good works" in the world will not save a group that chooses standard-brand commitment to old ideas, old systems, old forms of life in a world that needs reckless risk in behalf of new ones.

Religious life as we knew it is clearly dead. The only life left in it is what lives in the hearts of the members and is heard in the heart of the world.

Age, they want us to believe, blocks the life within us, makes it impossible for us to respond, dampens our effect, and denies us the right to move where we are needed. Tell that to Sarah and to Abraham, to Dorothy Day and Mother Teresa, to Bede Griffith and Dom Helder Camara. No, age is not our problem. Our problem is agedness and atrophy of soul, whatever our age. Our problem is that, schooled in a spirituality of silence and success, we have lost sight of the spirituality of risk. Yet, if this time is to lead to the next, then the life most staid of all must become a hotbed of risk, not only in member after member but in congregation after congregation. That is the very purpose of this time, of our time. That is the measure of religious life in our time. It is on this that our whole lives will be judged, in fact. It is time for new life in old age, and age, as every religious knows only too well, is no excuse for not living. It is time for living to the hilt. Nothing else, in fact, will make for sanctity now.

"Tell us about the place of risk in the spiritual life," the disciples said. So the Zen master told the story of the peasants who were taken by cargo plane month after month to work on the Burma road. The flight was long and the work was boring, so the men took to playing cards as they were flown from site to site. But since they had no money, they decided that the person who lost would be required to throw himself out of the airplane without a parachute. "Why, that's horrible!" the disciples gasped. "Ah, yes," the master said, "but it certainly made the game more exciting."

The message is clear: There is nothing in life more meaningful than gambling with our lives. In fact, isn't that why disciples become disciples in the first place?

6.

The Spirituality of Diminishment

Scripture is one long ledger of small people in contest with great groups who overpower them, overwhelm them, outnumber them and often seem to destroy them entirely. The Israelites in Egypt suffer slavery. David wrests Goliath. The exiles, marched out of Jerusalem after the fall of the temple, endure humiliation. Joseph, abandoned by his own brothers, knows isolation. Ruth, widowed in a male world, withstands abandonment. Esther, separated from the Jewish people and taken to the court of the Persian king, faces death. Judith, left to confront the warrior Holofernes alone, bears the hopes of the whole society on her back. One after another after another, they confront forces too mighty for them and survive to begin again.

But whatever the biblical connotations, powerlessness, smallness and weakness are not images we cherish either in this culture or this world. More than that, they are not roles we accept with equanimity. In the first place, Christendom, persecuted in its beginnings, flourished in the Western world nevertheless – and Christian institutions with it. The Christian church grew powerful and privileged, rich and politically influential. All of Europe breathed Catholic breath, and when not exclusively Catholic, almost exclusively Christian at least.

Size mattered and size triumphed. Powerlessness was not a favorite ecclesiastical pose.

Nor has the counting of souls and converts stopped to this day. Every year the church records the number of recent converts, the parishes newly formed. The church, herald of humility and keeper of the crucifixion, has given up its temporal power and privileged positions in Western society only slowly and with great reluctance, all scriptural figures notwithstanding.

The secular Western world itself, expeller of Goths and masters of colonies, does not take easily to loss either. The race for ascendancy rages to this day in every field: economics, commerce, science, military might, even sport and the international politics that surround what used to be games and what passes for play.

We live in a competitive world that reckons value in numbers and measures its mark by its size. We stake our advertising claims on the dimensions of a thing rather than on its quality: "The largest institution of its kind," we crow. . . . "The most members in its group . . . the biggest graduation class in history . . . the most extensive system in the world." Our slogans talk of power and domination: "We're Number One," we teach. "The Leader of the Western World," we call ourselves. "We Try Harder," we say of the number two team on its way to being number one. Obviously we know almost nothing about the vitality of smallness, let alone the desirability of smallness. We know hardly anything about the hand of God in situations of despair. We know pitiably little about the power of a single person whose heart is on fire in contrast to the ineffectiveness of multitudes of apathetic ones. We specialize in size, not necessarily commitment.

No wonder religious life is so stunned by its recent loss of numbers. No wonder its value is being gauged in terms of its size. No wonder we are talking abut the surety of its decline when we should be talking about the effects of its diminishment, positive as well as negative.

The topic of diminishment begs for resolution. Much of the institutional depression surrounding religious life at the present time has to do with age and numbers. Yet when Moses led the Israelites into the desert, no one asked them if they thought there were enough of them to find their way across it unguided or whether or not the median age of the group was low enough for the trip. The expectation was simply that everyone would go to the new land with whatever they had to take with them, and that having done that, Yahweh would raise them up a mighty people. If there is any question of faith, any room for hope in religious life today, this is surely it.

This time around we are being called one by one, not to a giant gathering with a given work at a special place but to join the remnant who see the process itself of going on as essential to the keeping of the fire and fundamental to the meaning of the life.

Religious Life in Decline?

It is possible that women and men shrink from entering religious congregations today, regardless of the fact that they may feel drawn to celibate, communal lifestyles, for no other reason than because religious themselves consider the life "in decline," not simply in a state of transition. Religious themselves too often doubt that God can raise a sprout from old roots and build new fire from old coals. Religious themselves fail to see the relationship between the work of institutional expansion and the waning of real religious witness. Religious themselves, perhaps, respond more with resignation to the loss of the old rather than with an abiding sense of stalwart sacrifice for the sake of whatever newness is meant to come out of this period. Religious themselves are demanding a glimpse of Canaan before they will agree to give up Egypt altogether. Religious themselves fail to understand that religious life is not a numbers game, not a security blanket, not an exercise in elitist establishmentarianism. On the contrary. It may be exactly at the point of highest productivity, greatest social acceptance, clearest success, widest scope and deepest institutional involvement that religious life goes most astray.

Religious life to be valid does not require a cast of thousands. It does not depend on hordes of people to prove its value. It was never meant to be a phalanx of faceless people, a world unto itself, an assembly line of anonymous, invisible, interchangeable parts. Religious life at its best is nothing more, perhaps, than a sentry on the wall, a bugler at dawn, a lamplighter at night, a candle on a far hill,. They are simple tasks, these, all very reflective and solitary and singular positions. All of them can easily be done, as scripture suggests, "two by two," with an eye to holding one another up, helping one another on, goading one another from place to place in order to speak where the voice of Scripture has been muted or has come up missing entirely.

What religious life needs at the present time, then, is a *spirituality of diminishment*, the understanding that the function of religious life is to be voice and call, presence and prophet to the world, not a labor force. Not even for the church.

"Never doubt that a small group of people can change the world, " the noted anthropologist Margaret Mead wrote. "Indeed that is all that ever has." There was only one Gandhi and a meager band of disciples, one Martin Luther King and a few personal advisors, one Thomas Merton and a handful of like-minded friends, but in every case the influence of these few far outranked their numbers. Quality, not quantity, marked their presence. Substance, not the size of the group, brought attention to their message and their message to the forefront of society. They were voices speaking to the hearts of the world around them about the questions few others were willing to address. They talked truth in a world that lied to

itself, called itself free and enslaved millions, called itself just
and imposed injustice on the world, called itself peace-loving
and treated the defenseless with ruthless force. Their power
was not in numbers or they would never have begun their
separate works, let alone succeeded. But they were an unusual
breed in a society that counts security in megatons, riches in
wealth, and success in numerical ratings. In this world, smallness and failure are synonyms.

While a world engorged with goods at the top and barren
to the bone at the bottom struggles to understand the place
and demand for diminishment, religious life stands in a position to model it. And resists. And uses the same standards
as the rest of the world to account for meaning and purpose
and effectiveness and status. So consumed are we as a church,
as a culture, as congregations by the seductiveness of numbers
that a spirituality of diminishment, a call to poverty of spirit,
escapes us entirely. We see as failure what may be our very
strength. We count as death what may well be new life within
us. We bemoan our dwindling numbers like Gideon who
thought the size of his army was more important to the defeat
of the enemy than the presence of God in the enterprise.

Because membership figures have shrunk, we count
ourselves useless instead of realizing that now, in us too, as
in Gideon, the Spirit can really make God's power known.
We evaluate every religious congregation in the world by the
number of members they had in 1950, as opposed to the size
of the roster in the year 2000. We assume without proof that
size and age are the marks of effectiveness, a motley band of
Israelites and the woman Sarah to the contrary.

The spirituality of diminishment, on the other hand,
contains within itself the challenge to trust insecurity and the
strength to divest ourselves of all the professional
accouterments we once took for granted – professional
preparation, public support systems, steady resources, clear
goals, the rewards of seniority, and institutional appreciation.

It demands the courage to go on bereft of those things to which we had become accustomed: nice, acceptable positions in clearly defined ministries under comfortable and socially approved conditions. It requires that we give up the idea of coasting into retirement on steadily decreasing responsibilities. It demands the kind of commitment our foundresses and founders brought to the altar – work without stint, trust without reason, prayer without ceasing, hope without end.

The spirituality of diminishment implies that we will go on without promise of success, with no memorials raised to our efforts, with no institutions to mark our accomplishments, with no respect for age, with no certainty that any one at any time will come behind us to complete the work, let alone hordes of people with unquestioning minds. Indeed, like Gideon at the walls of Jericho, we have pathetically few resources for a task far beyond us and the command to do it anyway. Surely the virtue of conformity never matched it for raw faith.

But we are not alone in the process. The whole Western world stands doomed to the throes of divestment, required to do more with less, if the peoples of the world are to flourish, if the planet itself is to survive. At this moment in history, diminishment is not a sign of failure, a sad preamble to death. It is, if we are to believe the voice of science, the warnings of ecologists, the very stuff of new life. If religious are the only people in society for whom the virtue of diminishment is impossible, the integrity of the past is as much in question as the authenticity of the present. Whatever have we been about? What did all the exercises and asceticisms of the past really teach us? What have our whole lives been about? If we cannot respond to the discipline of diminishment now, as once we lived with vigor the development of congregational institutions, we will certainly have missed the moment. We will have foregone, perhaps, the very time for which we came to religious life in the first place, the God-moment beyond all others, the holy time more purifying than any other. The problem will not be that the old form of religious life failed; the problem will be that we failed at the very moment that could have been the most valuable, the most real, the most sacred of our religious lives, the moment in which we were asked to give our whole life to what has little if any promise of success, simply because God wills it and it is right. If religious life in the past was worth anything at all, surely it should have been able to prepare us for this moment above all others before us.

The Faith to Dismantle

It is one thing to build a thing up; it is another thing entirely to have the faith to dismantle it with divine abandon, to give it up, to let it go, to throw ourselves in the arms of a God who, behold, is "making all things new."

The abrupt reduction of congregational size has brought religious life the opportunity to begin to live in new ways with new insights and new appreciations. Never before in the recent history of religious life, for instance, has it been so clear how important older members are to the group, or how competent younger people are. Everybody counts now. Everybody is unique gift now. Everybody weighs double now. As a result, both the level of maturity and the sense of ongoing life and formation have increased in communities across the world. Mechanisms designed to bring order to large groups – small representative chapters, rigid community schedules, institutional placements – have given way to more personal processes, to genuine appreciation and discovery of individuals and their very separate impact in both the group and in society itself.

The old assumptions about the need for parental authority and the virtue of feminine dependence and the need to control the activities of what was considered a herd of barely adult children have faded. In their place have arisen groups of self-directing, highly productive, womanly women who keep one eye on God and one eye on life at all times, who model the community of strangers that is the world, who believe that religious life is a very individual event designed to make groups fearlessly charismatic rather than simply functional. We can no longer hide behind the eminence of our institutions to be the stamp and measure of our own meaning. We must take our own vows quite seriously, more seriously than ever before, perhaps. We must bend every effort in us to be exactly what we say we are. Indeed, thanks to diminishment, religious life has come alive again. But not for itself alone.

Talk about solidarity with the poor must start with a respect for the kind of solidarity that comes out of knowing our own vulnerability. If religious communities stay bloated with members and insulated by security in a world where millions feel isolated and alone and under siege, how can they ever know the meaning of the poverty they say they are setting out to relieve? If religious do not know the feeling of powerlessness, they cannot understand how it is that two-thirds of the world live in the rage of powerlessness or the despair of powerlessness or the frustration of powerlessness or the faith of powerlessness everywhere? Women who do not understand the oppression of women cannot pretend to identify with the oppressed. People who have never known the effects of aging cannot begin to understand the pain of ageism. Diminishment, in other words, certifies religious to become what they say they want to be – one of the little ones, one of the simple ones, one of the humble ones, one of the dispossessed. Diminishment, if we allow it, if we embrace it, if we see it for the spiritual discipline it is, can save us from making a playschool out of religious life. Diminishment, the sense of smallness that comes from handing ourselves over to the immensity of God, from doing what cannot possibly succeed without the empowering presence of God, can make religious life real again to the point of pain.

The only question is, what will religious do with their newly found smallness that will hearten the poor around them who watch and look and see with interest how it is that the high and mighty become low again?

The Negative Effects

As cleansing and energizing as the positive effects of diminishment may be, however, the negative effects of diminishment pose equally serious threat to the meaning of the moment. It is so easy to give up when the forces seem so unbalanced and the venture feels so futile. Then, the temptation rises in a wild wave to give in to the systems around us, to succumb to the death of purpose. Given the decline in numbers, we excuse ourselves from the struggle. Or we become cynical about new efforts, new things, new prayer forms, new moments, new ideas. Or we deny the present situation entirely and settle down to wait for the return of another age. It is a serious moment in the life of the soul. It barters a lifetime of commitment. It makes a mockery of the gospel life.

As we see the old resources crumble around us, the old institutions lose their luster and their glory, the old social situation dry up and blow away, our own perspective begins to shift. The life struggle of religious commitment that used to be taken for granted, done with ease, in fact, looms larger than possible, larger than acceptable. The idea of starting over to do new work with new energy wearies us to the bone. Without the numberless numbers of candidates, the great, stable systems, public approval and parochial support, the question of who we are and what we do gnaws at the heart and leaves us arid of soul.

But this is a great moment for those whose souls are still alive with God. Diminishment requires more life of us than we have ever known before. It leads us to be ourselves, to give everything we've got, to know the power of God at work in us far beyond our own strength, far beyond our own vision. Diminishment gives us the opportunity, the reason, the mandate to examine our lives, to begin again, to dredge up what is best in us, to spill it recklessly across the canvas of the earth, to bank within us one more time the fires of commitment. Diminishment, arch-teacher of the soul, seals the entire enterprise. We know now that we are no more about our own work than were David, Joseph, Ruth, Esther, Judith, the Israelites in the desert or the exiles in Babylon. No, diminishment throws us back, whole and entire, small and trusting, aflame and afire, on God. And a life in God is anything but dead. It is glory beyond glory beyond glory.

Wax and wane it will, one always in the service of the other. The monastics say it this way:

> A pilgrim was walking along a road when one day he passed what seemed to be a monk sitting in a field. Nearby, men were working on a stone building.
>
> "You look like a monk," the pilgrim said.
>
> "I am that," said the monk.
>
> "Who is that working on the abbey?"
>
> "My monks," said the man. "I am the abbot."
>
> "Oh, that's wonderful," the pilgrim said. "It's so good to see a monastery going up.
>
> "We're tearing it down," the abbot said.
>
> "Tearing it down?" the pilgrim cried. "Whatever for?"
>
> "So we can see the sun rise at dawn," the abbot said.

To lose something is often to renew it.

7.

Following a Beckoning God

"Ideals are like the stars," Carl Schurz wrote. "We never reach them, but like the mariners of the sea, we chart our course by them." The search for perfect freedom, in other words, is a chimera. The attempt to live untethered in our own small worlds, untouched by the world around us, does not liberate life; it endangers it to its roots. Everyone needs something outside themselves to steer by, if for no other reason than without it, we will not know where to go. We will have energy without direction, the chaos of the soul.

Perhaps of all the questions facing religious life today, the most important, the most troublesome, is the question of fidelity itself. In a culture where change is swift and common, in a world where movement is global and given, in a society where three careers and two marriages are commonplace, the very notion of fidelity stretches us to the outside edge of meaning. Is there really any such thing as fidelity now? And why?

We think of the questions as new ones, bred out of a culture of social change and limitless options, but it doesn't take much reflection to realize that change, more than anything else perhaps, makes for the very essence of the spiritual life. The soul only grows as a result of the changes that tax and test our tolerance for the present, of the ability to find

God where God is rather than where we think God should be for us. Change of mind, change of heart, change of hopes, change of insights require us over and over again to sort through all the pseudo-certainties of our lives, keeping some things, altering others, discarding the rest of the notions that were once its convictions, its absolutes, the very staples of our souls. For religious of this latest period of history, the process of rediscovering the reason to go on, to exist even, has been one long unending enterprise. The question of fidelity to what and why, the clamorous questions that crowd in constantly for attention, follow at the heels of every other.

One thing for sure: what once we thought fidelity was all about has proven counterfeit.

Fidelity

The notion that fidelity cements a person in the past, accountable forever to decisions once made in good heart but without full insight or future experience, dies a dignified death in a period of rapid social change. Commitment to the past in a period such as this one simply sanctifies the quaint, if not the lethal. It does not necessarily sanctify the saintly, the challenges that face us in the present, the demands of the here and now. And everybody knows it. Those who set about to stop the pace around them in the name of fidelity to the past have nothing to offer a world which "the good old days" have passed by. The question is not to what were we asked to be faithful in the past. The question is to what must we be faithful in the present.

At the same time, too much change runs the risk of destabilizing the very ideas that undergird our lives and make change possible at all. When change is the high-priest of history, everything becomes suspect, everything becomes negotiable, nothing is taken for granted. Nothing is sacred. There is nothing to steer by, nothing to count on, nothing to be sure of, nothing to maintain. Turmoil sets in with a vengeance. Anomie, the loss of a sense of purpose in life, begins to corrode the soul. The feeling that anything is possible turns into the feeling that nothing is possible.

Ironic as it may seem, change depends on the notion that some things are changeless. We can change all the externals of life – where we live, what we wear, what we do, how we do it – and still be faithful as long as the internal definition of who we are and what we are about changes not at all. A marriage does not automatically dissolve simply because the children die before the parents. Police are no less police simply because they become plainclothes officers. Religious life is no less religious life simply because the mode of living it – the ministry, the life pattern, the schedule – changes. Conscious change relies for its success on the fact that in the course of it some things, important things, do not change at all, that something stabilizes us yet, that our feet rest on bedrock whatever the shifts in the world around us. And that is precisely where real fidelity begins.

Fidelity does not lie in refusing to change. Permanence is not a synonym for constancy. Fidelity lies in making whatever changes are necessary to bring us from the ideals out of which we have always operated in order to achieve those ideals toward which we have always striven. If service to the poor has been the ideal out of which the congregation emerged, then changing ministry – no matter how time-honored the work – when I discover that I am serving only those who can afford to get the services they need somewhere else, is the acme of fidelity, not betrayal of either the charism of the congregation or of my own which mirrors it. Fidelity manifests the truest part of us in process to the whole of us. Coming to wholeness by being faithful to the self and the inspiriting ideals we steer by means that we will never make fidelity our excuse not to become what we must most be.

But if real fidelity requires steadfast commitment to those values which direct and define us, which lie at the core of the soul like a lodestone, which transcend all others and measure our authenticity, then what is philosophically obvious begins to ring with a more ominous tone. Indeed, we do not enter religious life to be religious. We enter religious life to seek God. And if that is true, then we can truly be religious only as long as participation in the institute enables in us both the single-minded search for God and the success of the seeking in our own lives. If a congregation itself warps the notion of fidelity by maintaining what was for its own sake rather than making possible what must be for the sake of the Gospel now, it is the congregation that has ceased to be faithful, not the members who prod it to fulfillment. "If the Church itself should become an obstacle to our salvation," Thomas Aquinas writes, "we would be required to leave the Church." That is the essence of fidelity, to be willing to forego anything that makes the best in us impossible. To make perpetual that which is not worthy of eternal pursuit and everlasting preservation is not a virtue.

Fidelity is not stability of place; it is stability of heart. Fidelity goes wherever it must to follow the star that it dare not lose at the risk of spending life forever off-compass. Fidelity means being willing to change in order to remain the same.

The tragedy is that over the years we have wrenched the idea of *fidelity* to mean *moral perfection* as well as perpetuity, as if there were such a thing. To be faithful to the vows came to mean never to "break" them, as if they were fragile glasses on a teetering shelf. To be faithful, the teaching implied, meant never to balk at an order, never to buy things, never to wrestle with the burdens and blessings of human love, never to question, never to pay the price of real commitment. Such a sad and dwarfed idea it became, this being faithful to rules that never allowed the possibility of being faithful to the self and its questions, the self and its struggles, the self and its coming to wholeness. Fidelity began to be defined as a commitment to eternal adolescence, to foreclosures on human development, rather than to the scarred and scary process of growing to adulthood one step at a time. To grow up, with all the trial and error implied in such an intricate process, became a matter of grave disregard rather than a reason for rejoicing. But surely that smacks of limited understanding of both human nature and human good. Or wasn't David, despite being full of anger and lust, faithful to the God who called him beyond them? Was Jonah, full of the struggle that came with his pettiness and cowardice, any less faithful to Yahweh in the end than someone without those problems? When God commanded Jonah to go to the people of Nineveh, something Jonah did not want to do, Jonah bought himself first a ticket to Tarshish and went in exactly the opposite direction, a reaction which at first looks like a shocking infidelity on his part. Yet, it was in Tarshish where Jonah finally discovered the major lesson of his life, that escape from God was not possible! Was Peter's fidelity any less real for the fact that, under pressure and choosing for his own security and status, he first denied his association with Christ? On the contrary, it was in following another road for awhile that he discovered how small a god he was unto himself in comparison to the Christ whom he had professed to follow. Clearly, fidelity to the process of the growth of God in us and the achievement of a legalistic kind of "perfection" or "commitment" are not the same thing. There are twists and turns in every life meant to take us ultimately to the one point toward which we turn: the heart of God and the God of our hearts.

It is a shocking concept, this notion that fidelity does not lie in standing in place but in consistently moving toward whatever brings us to more and more wholeness of heart, certainty of soul, clarity of mind and integrity of behavior until we finally know deep in our deepest selves what stars really guide us. Fidelity is the ability to move freely through life because of the unwavering ideals that call us on from wherever we are to where we must be if we are ever to achieve and maintain those ideals at all. Fidelity is not the state of never making a mistake. Fidelity is the state of never staying in one. Was Moses "faithful" when he killed the Egyptian? Was David "faithful" when he took Nathan's wife? Not at all, if fidelity is a synonym for perfection. Decidedly yes, however, if fidelity means working life through to the end, taking nothing for granted, struggling till the struggle ends.

Question the Ultimate Value

Fidelity requires that we question the ultimate value of everything along the way – ourselves and everything we do, most of all. Fidelity is not the fine art of arresting growth in mid-air. Fidelity is what, when we test it, makes us think, makes us decide, makes us choose between what we can be, what we are being, and what, ultimately, we want to be.

The spiritual life does not depend on arresting growth at the point of choice; fidelity makes growth possible by forcing us to choose and choose again, weaving this way and that through life, reaching by means of the present, confused and alluring as it may be, to the purpose for which we were made. And often we fail. And often only failure can teach us what we really need to know about life. Being faithful to the continued need to choose between things, between things that are good as well as bad, so that we can commit ourselves always to the better for us, rather than to simply the adequate, tests fidelity to the core.

Commitments take the static out of life. By committing ourselves to one thing instead of another, we get standards to steer by and the space to become. Commitments force us to be what we say we want to be. Commitments make us responsible for others as well as ourselves. Commitments test the mettle out of which we're made.

Having chosen for one thing, we are free then to allow it to test us and stretch us and bring us to our best selves. Commitments show us a way, they focus us, they constrain us from a confusion of choices, all equally good, perhaps, but all with conflicting expectations. Commitment keeps us in place, in other words, until our souls, tried by fire and fired by life, expand to their full measure.

Commitments have personal purposes as well as social ones. In order to learn what life is meant to teach us, we must keep ourselves from running away from life when it gets hard, when it finally begins to demand something from us, when it asks far more from us than we ever expected to be able to give. Fidelity is not standing in place for the sake of being able to say we stood there. Fidelity is the potter's kiln of life where, tried by heat and flame, we change into shapes and glazes of which we never dreamed.

Fidelity is not fidelity, then, until it's tried. Fidelity really happens at those moments when, in our unfaithfulness, we come to understand most clearly exactly what we have lost in the failing and choose it still. "There is no failure," Kin Hubbard writes, "except in no longer trying. There is no defeat except from within; no really insurmountable barrier save our own inherent weakness of purpose." Fidelity to purpose, whatever the pitfalls of the search, makes of life a miracle that happens daily.

For religious in this period of history, fidelity has something to do with being willing to find new ways of being in the world so that the old desire to serve God and God alone in a society of false and pluriform gods can live anew. Fidelity for religious of any day is clearly not blind pledge to past forms of the lifestyle, to past standards of perfection, to past obligations whose prophetic value has gone silent. To maintain things that are counterproductive of human growth,

others as well as our own, or made up of spiritual exercises
that no longer nourish the spiritual life is to sin against fidelity
in the most faithless of ways. What we must be faithful to is
the beckoning God, who goes before us into human history
healing what is wounded, raising up what is good in us for
all to see and calling us to do the same.

Fidelity and Endurance

Fidelity and Endurance are ideas in opposition. When I stay
with something that is not good for me simply to prove to
myself that I can endure what I can no longer love and
through which I can no longer come to fullness of life, I do
no favors to anyone, least of all to my own search for God.
Fidelity is not a style of life that suffers in silence for the sake
of suffering. We are only truly faithful to what we are when
we pursue the life of it with passion, sometimes with pain, but
always with a willingness to pay the price, whatever the cost
of coming to know our own smallness – as Moses did, as David
did, as Jonah did – because life lived well is worth the cost of
it.

The real challenge to fidelity today, then, arises out of
the need to determine and define to what we must be faithful.
Is fidelity measured by our commitment to a congregation
that has long ago gone to seed, and goes through the motions
of a religious life long past, but has yet to muster the faith it
takes to produce a religious life that finds God and frames
God in this time? Is fidelity described by our degree of agree-
ment with the tenets of a church that must also be about the
process of finding new answers to new questions, instead of
pawning off the past in the name of perfection? Is fidelity
what we give when, in the name of being faithful, we refuse
to think with the rest of the thinking world about the questions
that will define the future of life on this planet and the
authenticity of life in this church: abortion, euthanasia, nu-

clear weaponry, papacy, collegiality, sexism, and science on a rampage – as if Jesus did not think newly about lepers and sin, women and life, priests and people, God and pharisees?

On the contrary. What we were born to be faithful to is no institution whatsoever, however exalted its claims. Fidelity, purely and simply, pursues from one stage, one place, one project to another, only the mind of God and the passionate presence of the Gospel in a world more comfortable with creeds than with religion, more familiar with the church than with the Christ, more committed to charity than to justice, more enmeshed in oppression than equality, more devoted to maintaining the faith of the fathers by outlawing female pronouns in sacred texts than they are to the liberating impetus of the Good News itself. Indeed, we must watch carefully to what we are faithful for fear fidelity undoes us all.

"We build statues out of snow," the poet Walter Scott wrote, "and weep to see them melt." In our fidelities lie our disillusionments. If we lose sight of what we're about in this period of the keeping of the coals, it may be because we never did really know or, knowing, were faithful to the wrong things. If our fidelity to religious life in this period means anything at all, surely it means being faithful to its participation in the Mystery – whatever the system – and faithful to our own pursuit of it, not settling down and turning into straw, not confusing inertia with an ongoing commitment. Just because we do not do anything that changes direction does not mean that we are being faithful to anything. On the contrary.

Fidelity is our answer to the God who is faithful. That does not mean that God rejects change. It simply means that God is with us through every change, through every turn of direction toward the home of the heart. Whatever change demands in our life means that we must, through it all, simply be with God, remain in God, seek God at the core of it, the foundation upon which our lives and all life's changes rest. Fidelity is what sustains us when reason does not. When everything around us tells us that what we invested in is now not worth it, fidelity takes over and enables us to carry what can no longer carry us.

Fidelity and Tenacity

We must then be careful to distinguish between fidelity and tenacity. Fidelity isn't the fine art of gritting our teeth and staying at something simply for the sake of staying at it. Fidelity implies that we must work at being what we say we will be, that we continue to give ourselves to it even when it seems to be giving nothing back, provided that it is still worth the price of our lives, provided that it remains a star to steer by, provided that its end for us is the living God and not a cheap facsimile. It is important always to remember that what we are faithful to is the faithful God. We must never be faithful to a thing for its own sake or fidelity will become an idol in itself, disheartened and bogus.

The truth is that things change, things get corrupted, things fail, things die. What does not die is the commitment to stay faithful to the search, to the quest that leads us like the North Star through life.

There are obstacles to fidelity that need to be uprooted from the religious soul. Rigidity is an obstacle to fidelity. Unchanging commitment to non-change flies in the face of the Holy Spirit. Anything else may well arrest our own development, stunt us and leave us at the end of life hardly having lived at all.

Insincerity is an obstacle to fidelity. When we don't do our part, when we stop praying, when we stop trying, when we stop dreaming the dream of the life itself, that's infidelity. When we stop believing that this great commitment to the pursuit of the presence of the Spirit in this way can be, should be, is, for me, the most direct route to the living God, that is the greatest unbelief of all. It is not fidelity to change direction simply because the one I know deep in my heart that I should be on got difficult to continue.

The fruits of fidelity, of keeping an eye on the heights but being willing to slog through soaked plains to get there, defy simple description. They dance and sing. They are freedom from rigidity, freshness of thought, faith in God, and fortitude under stress. Fidelity is the willingness to perdure in crisis, to see a thing through, to work it out because working it out, making it work, is something worth the grappling with. Fidelity is staying with a thing, however difficult the doing at times, because I would be less myself if I did not. In the Sayings of the Desert Monastics, Amma Syncletica's teaching on the subject leaves little doubt about the role of fidelity in the human life: "If you happen to live in a community," she taught her disciples, "do not move to another place, for it will harm you greatly. If a bird leaves her eggs, they never hatch. So also the monk and the nun grow cold and dead in faith by going from place to place." To be cold and dead in faith deadens all of life itself. To be passionately alive in the faith is the purpose of religious fidelity.

The miracle was not that God parted the waters of the Red Sea. The miracle was that once parted, the people had fidelity enough to be willing to walk trustingly through the mountainsides of water. That is our task as well. The faithful person moves beyond fear of the present with its challenges to accept a future full of possibility. Fidelity knows that there is nothing to fear. This is God's world. The questions and changes of the present age, of our personal lives, are God's work and so ours as well. To ignore them in the name of being faithful to the past can only be the height of infidelity. In the retreat to commitment – a clinging to what was in order to avoid what must be – lies a coward's cross.

When the world as we have known it breaks down, when life as we have lived it fails to work for us anymore, fidelity demands that we see the new questions as God's call to grow, either further into the new situation or deeper into the old one. But grow we must or we risk remaining adolescents all our adult lives.

Fidelity demands that we stay true to the search itself, brooking no fixed stops along the way. The poet James Russell Lowell understood the real function of fidelity in life. "Not failure, but low aim, is crime," he wrote. When we refuse life's questions in favor of intellectual safety, social approval or personal security, we have failed to be faithful to life, no matter how faithful we claim to be.

In his "Tales of a Magic Monastery," Theophane Boyd writes the parable that exposes the spiritual life for all its messiness. The tale reads:

> I had just one desire – to give myself completely to God. So I headed for the monastery. An old monk asked me, "What is it you want?"
>
> I said, "I just want to give myself to God."
>
> I expected him to be gentle, fatherly, but he shouted at me: "NOW!"
>
> I was stunned. He shouted again. "NOW!" Then he reached for a club and came after me. I turned and ran. He kept coming after me, brandishing his club and shouting, "NOW, NOW."
>
> That was years ago. He still follows me, wherever I go. Always that stick, always that "NOW!"

It is in the now that fidelity and faith meet the forces of life. No religious life that refuses either can really be religious life. Here we struggle. Here we grow. Here we are meant to be, in the process of process, not in some fixed cocoon proclaiming our disinterest in life, eschewing its ongoing questions, insisting that anesthetizing the soul is a virtue – and all of it in the name of the God who is ever new.

8.

To Become the Flame

The tradition tells us that someone asked Abba Anthony, "What must I do to please God?" And the old man replied, "Pay attention to what I tell you. Whoever you may be, always have God before your eyes; whatever you do, do it according to the testimony of the holy Scriptures; in whatever place you live, do not easily leave it. Keep these three precepts and you will be saved." The story captures the dimensions of religious life too easily forgotten. Religious life is about seeking God, doing the Gospel and persisting in the pursuit of the two. Religious life captures our heart, focuses our mind and stabilizes our soul for the single-minded search for the living reign of God. Whatever religious dedication may look like to the world around it, under no conditions should religious life be confused with membership in a religious institution. Most of all, religious life is not an institution, a kind of church machine designed simply to provide a base for social service. In fact, social service in its own right is not what inspires religious commitment at all. It demonstrates it, yes; it fulfills it, true; it makes it authentic, of course, but it does not inspire it; it does underlie it; it does not define it. Religious life is a very personal, a very human, a very spiritual, a very life-absorbing thing. Otherwise, a person could simply be professionally certified for it, or hired into it, or publicly solicited for short-term service. The truth is, however, that religious life either fits a person or it doesn't. If it doesn't, then all the talking in the world about sanctity or fidelity or commitment cannot make a bit of difference to the person for whom the fit is not real. If it does, no amount of change can damp its spirit.

No, religious life is not a system devised for the recruiting of church professionals. Religious life is a lifestyle, a time-honored way of being Christian in the world. It is simply one form of the Christian life among several, true. But it is its own form. Distinct from all others in style, devoted to the Christian pursuit, designed for those with a passion for the mystery of life, it concentrates exclusively on plumbing and proclaiming the Good News that Jesus is, Jesus saves and Jesus cares. For all of us. For everything. For both people and planet. Always. And it does so not simply by bringing a service to the world but by being a faithful presence within it that sets out to speak a gospel language in the mother tongue.

Religious life is the story of the whole of creation writ large in a single person's life. Those who foolishly expect or romantically assume that life in a religious community makes for life without the pressures of the real world know little about the life and less about the human responsibility to co-creation. They make a myth of a gospel that casts out demons and challenges pharisees, suffers temptation and raises up figures who show the greatest fragility under the least of pressure. Life in religious community taps them all. People who come to religious life bring the demons of their souls, the need for challenge, the most tenacious of tempta-tions and the most vulnerable of weaknesses. People who come to religious life are not people who are running away from themselves, however. They are people who set out to take life with both hands, to face it squarely, to live it to the hilt.

Christian life in religious community is for people who want to be fully alive. It is not for people who choose to go through life half-anesthetized spiritually, dulled psychologically, and mostly dense to the rest of the world around them. Thrown back upon themselves, committed to a life full of strangers, adrift in the currents and phases of the spiritual life and responsive to some small voice of formless faith within them, religious live a life full of hope and steeped in human struggle, not a semi-comatose excursion into spiritual isolation where contention never touches and self-knowledge never penetrates.

If we attempt to use religious life to get away from people, we aspire in vain to protect for ourselves what must not ever, in a world full of the rejected and the refugee, be protected. We do not come to religious life to isolate ourselves from the Gospel we talk about. If anyone must, it is the religious who must take them all, these outcasts, into their lives, every last, difficult, despicable one of them. A person does not come to religious life to play poor while basking in security. On the contrary, religious life strips us down, each of us together and alone, to the essentials of life so that we can, finally, be filled up with things beyond things. We do not come to religious life because we suffer from indecisiveness and cannot function without direction. We come so that together with others we can listen for the Spirit in voices that are not our own. Religious life is not easy but it is also not unreal, not quixotic, not bizarre.

All the Life We Have

To live a religious life takes all the life we have. To live a religious life takes the heart of a hermit, the soul of a mountain climber, the eyes of a lover, the hands of a healer, and the mind of a rabbi. It requires total immersion in the life of Christ and complete concentration on the meaning of the

Gospel life today. It presumes a searing presence. Maybe that's where things began to go wrong.

Before the 13th century and the mushrooming of canon law, religious promised an amorphous and largely unofficial kind of commitment to live an intensely spiritual life, to turn toward God alone in making life choices, to stay right-minded in a world awash in itself, to become people of the scriptures. Religious sought God and God alone, and in the doing of it became the wisdom figures, the gurus, the spiritual directors of a society so steeped in the secular that the sacred had become invisible, so bereft of the memory of the divine that secular concerns consumed the human condition. Then, however, in a climate newly enamored of universities and formal education and philosophical disputations, and faced with the decadence of religious communities that had become religious resorts for the daughters and sons of the wealthy, the concept of "vows" emerged. The life began to be defined and theologized and regulated. Soon, the "evangelical counsels" of poverty, chastity and obedience became the criteria and the measure of the spiritual life. And with them, over the centuries, came the spiritual manuals and the categories and canons that set out to control behavior. But the process smothered the spirit of the life, as well. Slowly but surely, religious commitment began to be reduced to a series of activities when what was needed was more an attitude of mind and a promise of prophetic presence. Soon, religious became more what they did than what they were, than what they saw, than what they thought.

What's worse, the Christian community at large – sometimes religious most of all – wondered at the yardsticks used to measure the authenticity of the life. The theological questions with which religious now concerned themselves, formed themselves, accused themselves became downright inane, pathetic, sniveling, meant to serve the greatest of spiritual ideals, surely, but beneath the dignity of a spiritual adult. The great issues of the religious life became a series of inconsequential little questions: How much money did poverty permit a religious to carry in the pocket at any one time? Was it disobedient to contest a superior's information? Was the adherence to house customs of the essence of religious obedience or not? Were colored bedspreads acceptable in the bedroom of a nun? Was humility measured by the tilt of the headgear? Was friendship a threat to a person's religious life? How many books, statues, records, tapes, habits, shoes, could a religious own and not violate the vow of poverty? Could a religious get toothpaste without the express permission of her superior? The list went on – and it got worse as it went.

But have no doubt about it: the list was not ineffective. Life without autonomy over the most basic of life matters made for a spiritual culture of great security and great anxiety as well. It also made for spiritual narcissism. It made for holy childishness. It made for self-centeredness, masked as virtue but dangerously close to the point of the neurotic. It made religious life a sincere but pale shadow of a gospel full of unacceptable miracles and uneven matches between the keepers of the system and the cullers of hearts. It reduced a giant of a life to the dimensions of a dwarf. Spiritual children now walked in the way where once only disciples and martyrs, brave men and strong women had been.

Any life that takes a person's whole life must surely be about more than that.

Perhaps it is time, then, to strip away the notion of religious life as an exhibit of three isolated codes of conduct and ask simply what kind of person, what kind of Christian life, would exist in the world if religious began again to see religious commitment in terms of spiritual attitudes rather than a code of personal behavior. Clearly, at the dawn of the 21st century, professing poverty, chastity and obedience in a world where poverty is a sin against justice, chastity is an academic question, not a given, and obedience is bred more by the military than by a culture that values independence, makes religious life more suspect than impressive. To maintain that approach only cheapens the life beyond all justification for it, turns it into some kind of institutionalized cult, limits its spiritual power.

The Search for God

The search for God is a lifelong process of shaping the soul, not a short-term routine of religious exercises. Religious life is about the unleashing of spiritual presence in a world lost in the mundane, not about the perpetuation of an arcane lifestyle for its own sake. Religious congregations were not founded to be anthropological museums. They are made up of real people, all adult, doing real things for important reasons.

Religious life is the story of the prophets – ordinary people with theophanous insight who had to become something new themselves in order to bring new insight to others.

Religious life, in other words, requires us first to convert ourselves. It is the ground of growth, not a lifestyle for the keeping of customs. It demands that we be totally up to date, not hopelessly out of touch. Until religious are converted to the mind of God alive and present in the now, what good can they possibly be for anyone else, no matter what kind of services they may perform on the side? Religious life is not about ministry; it is about developing a heart and mind that come to see life as it is and so rouse us to live differently ourselves because of it.

Religious, like everyone else alive, are people of their times. That's what makes them dangerous. That's also what makes them potentially insipid. The fact is that religious are not simply to be people of the world. They are also to be consciously, continually and consistently people of God, people who pursue the mind of God and people who proclaim it, whatever the cost to themselves.

To understand the role of conversion in religious life is to understand the ancient concept of "chosenness." The Hasidim put it this way: "Once upon a time a rabbi was asked how it felt to be a rabbi. "Well," the rabbi said, "I began to understand it better when I worked in the sheepfold. There every tenth lamb was chosen for service in the temple just by reason of being number ten. And just that way was I chosen to be rabbi as well." No one is "chosen," in other words, because they are better than anyone else for anything and everyone is "chosen" for something. Everyone has some internal disposition that suits them for what must be done in them, that calls them to it, that confirms them in it, that marks them for that service. Like people with perfect pitch for music and people with manual dexterity for crafts and people with an artist's eye for photography, there is in some people a highly honed commitment to the spiritual dimensions of the human endeavor and the things of God, primarily and alone. It is this heightened religious sensibility that calls a person, that leads a person to concentrate exclusively on the development of the spiritual component of human life.

But even though something is natural to us – a love for children, a passion for art, a seeker's soul and a visionary's vision – does not mean that because the capacity is real it is also ready. It only means that it is available for shaping. Then conversion begins.

Religious life takes the soul of the seeker and sands away its outer layers to its center, so that what we are seeking we can see and what we are hungry for we can taste, and what we are pursuing we can become, and what Good News we are full of we can finally say for all the world to hear.

The function of religious life, clearly, is first to take our very ordinary selves, to steep them in the scriptures and then to hold them taut against the measure of the one who withstood both synagogue and state for the sake of the Word of God. The life of conversion converts, first of all, ourselves. Then, perhaps, through that transformation it transforms the tiny circle of life in which we stand, as well, so that through one person at a time, in each of us, the world may be returned to the One who made it, whole and entire, full of life, full of fire.

Conversion

Conversion is the process of coming to see the world differently than culture and comfort and the desire to control entice us into seeing it. The question, of course, is: what is this way of being in the world that is called "religious life"? What's so different about it that can't be done just as well in any other form of Christian life? The answer, of course, at one level at least, is nothing. We are all called to the spiritual life, to conversion, to Christianity at its pristine best. This form of the Christian life, however, requires a specific focus, a clear and certain emphasis, a sure and common quality that makes it different from all others in style and clarity of presence.

This form demands the conversion in us of everything this world holds most dear. It requires a commitment to scaling parapets with the Jesus who was tempted and saying no again, loudly and with conviction, prophetically and with purpose, to the kind of power that disempowers others; no to profit-taking that flourishes on the backs of the poor; and no to relationships that seduce the innocent and exploit the unwary and twist the little ones of the world into shrunken instruments of personal satisfaction.

Freedom and perspective are the gifts of religious life to the world around it. Consumed by nothing but the reign of God, the religious it is who stands to see everything else most clearly precisely because of the distance they keep from it.

When beholden to no one and seduced by nothing, the religious stands free to call the conscience of the king. The presence of religious, real religious, is a dangerous thing in any society.

As the Chinese occupied Tibet, a Zen story tells, many of the soldiers showed great cruelty in regard to the subjugated peoples. The most chosen object of their atrocities were the monks. So as the foreign forces invaded villages, the monks fled to the mountains. When the Chinese invaders arrived in a particular village, the lieutenant of the advance troops reported "All the monks, hearing of your approach, Excellency, fled to the mountains . . ." The commander smiled, smugly proud of his fearsomeness. "All, that is, but one," the lieutenant continued quietly. The commander became enraged. He marched to the monastery and kicked in the gate. There in the courtyard stood the one remaining monk. The commander glowered at him. "Do you not know who I am? I am he who can run you through with a sword without batting an eyelash." And the monk replied: "And do you not know who I am? I am he who can let you run me through with a sword without batting an eyelash."

Indeed, the religious, free, detached, centered in God brings danger to a society. But first, of course, religious must in this day and age want to become something new. Religious must first be converted themselves.

But how and to what? If the spirituality of the past degenerated into codes and canons, rules and regulations, exercises and rituals, however good, however well-intentioned, what is the subject matter of conversion now? Is there anything left in this period that is the raw material of holiness?

9.

The Living Testimony

It is not easy to write about vows in this period of religious history. Many religious doubt their worth altogether and would, if they could, simply collapse the traditional promises into a commitment to the Gospel life or some similar formulation. Many more at least question their content if not their existence. Most religious who were formed before Vatican II give them much less attention now than they did then. Nor were vows an essential element of early religious life. The question becomes then, "Are the vows an important part of the spiritual life for contemporary religious or not?" And the answer may be a clear and firm, "Yes and no." No, if we use them as restrictions on life; yes, if we see them as attitudes toward life.

Since most religious who entered religious congregations after Vatican II have never had the vows reduced to a series of prescribed or forbidden behaviors, the vows may have a better chance in the future of becoming for the world what they were always meant to be: beacons, ideals, signs of hope to be lived in the here and now, in the public world as well as in the private life of the community.

But besides the question of whether there should be any such thing as the vows of religion or not, there is another question even more serious than the first: "Why, of all the things that a spiritual person could vow in life – prayer, service, ecumenism, ecology – do religious go on vowing poverty, chastity and obedience?" What could sound more arid? What could be less engaging? What could appear less developmental in a world where poverty is a major problem, chastity is no longer as much a protection against unwanted pregnancies as it is a virtue, and where obedience has been degraded to the point of no return by the perpetration of holocausts and genocide and political corruption? What is the spiritual use of what nobody cares about and nobody wants? If I pledge to go to the moon in this culture, people are in awe. If I commit myself to support a major civic development project, people are clear about their admiration. If I promise to give my life to pursuing the questions of modern science, people applaud. If I talk about being a religious, people are eager to understand the life and to encourage the new developments in it. But if I talk about committing my life to poverty, chastity and obedience, people hardly respond at all anymore. They're not impressed, they're not influenced, they're not as stirred as once they were at the thought of undertaking such a severe public witness to such important elements of life. For some reason, it seems, the vows have simply lost meaning, both within religious life and outside of it as well. But why? Is it the nature of the vows themselves that people question, or is it the way we apply the vowed life to modern life that makes them uncaring, that makes them skeptical about the value of spiritual promises that have no material meaning? Is the religious life simply a symbolic life or does it have substance enough to make it meaningful to the world around it?

The answers to all those questions depend, of course, on how religious themselves see the function of the vows in their own personal lives, and then in the life of the people in whose midst they pronounce them publicly. Vows, our most longstanding theologies on the subject tell us, are to be a public witness to Gospel values. A public witness. Something the public can see and take heart from, take hope from. The vows are not the private preserve of pious people who fear the world and therefore flee from it. The vows pledge us to give our lives to the things we're for, not to try to escape the things we're against.

But if that is the case, maybe the world has never needed these vows more than it needs them now. Provided we ourselves know what the vows mean for our time. Provided we ourselves live their meaning.

The Zen masters teach: "When a monk goes into a tavern, the tavern becomes his cell. And when a haunter-of-taverns goes into a cell, the cell becomes a tavern." We take with us wherever we go what we are, and what we are affects, for better or worse, for good or for little, the timbre and tone of the places we go. The meaning of religious commitment stands out far more clearly in this explanation of religious life as leaven, I think, than all the canonical definitions of poverty, chastity and obedience that have ever been written. In fact, just saying those words brings with them the waft of mothballs and a long, slow yawn.

Religious Poverty

What is religious poverty to people but a canonical game in a world where downright destitution is the curse of most of the children of the earth? What is chastity in a lonely and loveless life but the promotion of some kind of twisted constraint of heart in a world where repressed or exploited or warped sexuality now pervades the very air we breathe? What is obedience to those who are already oppressed except yet more humiliating subservience in a world where the autonomy of peoples is everywhere a heaving, national hope? What "witness" value, in other words, is security, isolation, and dependence when people everywhere find those things yokes to be broken, not values to be esteemed?

When religious poverty ceased to be real, and when non-chastity ceased to be so much a social peril with its threat of unwanted children, and when obedience gave way to "liberty, equality and fraternity" in a world bereft of kings and queens, that kind of religious life became more and more a kind of cardboard cutout of life, a series of empty exercises for religious martinets, all of them sincere, but all of them more and more out of touch with the needs of people, the undercurrents of the times that called all of society to the new demands of old virtues.

But religious life cannot continue to exist that way. What the world needs now, respects now, demands now, understands now is not poverty, chastity and obedience. It is generous justice, reckless love and limitless listening. Mechanical adherence to mechanical concepts leaves religious life sterile and empty, both for the people in it and the people outside of it as well. The world has too many plastic copies of the real thing already to begin to appreciate another one, even one that parades in the name of religion. Nor should it. If the scriptures show us anything, they show us the power of the real thing.

There was only one Abraham, one Moses, one Judith, one David, one Deborah and one Samaritan woman, all of them flawed, all of them fragile. Yet they turned their worlds upside down, not because they were quaint "symbols" of what might be but because they were the genuine article in a world in search of truth and direction. The disciples, too, were sent out only "two by two," not in great groups; but they completely changed the face of the Roman world, not because they were powerful but because they were fearlessly unfeigned, totally committed, relentlessly *bona fide.* They were what they said they were, not vacant imitations of it, however unfeigned. Codified vows in a world looking for virtue will not be enough to change the world. Virtue beyond vows, life lived above and beyond law for the sake of the world, rather than primarily for the sanctification of the self, can turn it upside down.

Religious life can no longer afford to be simply a figure of anything. It must be what it was in its beginnings. It must be the real thing: really attuned to poverty and its effects, really intent on a chastity that frees; really committed to hearing the voices of the entire world. Now, if religious life is going to be a gift in hard times, a living picture of the world for which the people wait, it must be what it says it is. It must be the real article now, the model of what must be but is not.

What a world awash with refugee camps and hungry children, beaten women and homeless men, Third-World debts and political policies aimed at balancing the budget at the expense of the people's needs is a religious life that vows to be what the world needs most: a reckless lover, a voice for the poor, a pursuer of truth. For only such things as this, for this kind of poverty, chastity and obedience only, does the present battered, exploited and poverty-stricken world wait and grieve and crave.

Spirituality

Spirituality is not the romantic rendering of a fanciful mysticism, an overdrawn religious imagination let loose upon the world to gush at it or scold at it or fuss at it. Spirituality is theology walking. Spirituality is what we do because of what we say we believe. What we dogmatize in creeds, spirituality enfleshes and what we enflesh is what we really believe. If, for instance, we believe that the Incarnation made all humanity holy, then we must be squarely on the side of those whose lives are undervalued, denigrated, or derided. If we believe in the eucharistic community, then we must share the bread of our lives with those who are truly hungry and the wine of our days with those whose hearts lack the joy of life. If we believe in Bethlehem, then we must listen for truth and be alert to revelation where truth and revelation may seem least likely to be. Most of all, we must finally accept the fact that the spiritual truth writ most plain right now is that religious life will not be saved by a new set of rules. Religious life can only be saved by being what it says it is, by doing what it is supposed to do, by becoming a new way of being in the world. Religious life must be about seeing what others do not see or saying what others may not say, for whatever reason, at whatever price. Religious must be about the great questions of life, not religious playschool or spiritual massage.

But that can only be done if religious live four-square in the present with hearts attuned to the here and now. Nice words, yes, but hard ones. If religious communities bring focus to the individualism, the exploitation and the engorgement around them, they may well find themselves walking a rough road, following a dark path, treading a lonely course. To find ourselves in question of things considered normal, acceptable, even desirable to the powerful and the privileged, barters all the respect, all the gentility to which we have become so accustomed in the days of our ascent to the Establishment.

It was not always so, however. When the fire was new and high, no amount of rejection deterred. Our forebears knew rejection and hostility in a society that wanted nothing of Catholic schools or Catholic institutions, or even of Catholics themselves, but they developed each of them regardless. They lived for God, not for social approval. They cared about the Gospel, not the law. They operated on faith, not on prudence. We, on the other hand, have too often lost the fine art of the "witness" we like so much to talk about. This time the scope of religious witness looms even larger than before. It is not the Catholic population alone to which religious life must now be committed if the Gospel in us is ever to ring true. This time it is the globe and all its people for whom we must speak if what we proclaim by our lives can possibly be affirmed by the scriptures, let alone validated by the vows. It is time again to be the kind of presence that lights a fire, it is time to become the flame. If only we did not cling to the shadows of past fires. If only we did not fear the heat of this one.

10.

A Call to Justice

Three elements of modern life pervade society today and call for a new kind of religious presence in special ways. *Engorgement, exploitation* and *oppression* keep humanity in bondage, while religious life stands at risk of giving itself over to praying prayers, eating regular meals, surrounding itself with "nice" people, doing basic institutional work and proving its spiritual worth by raising no questions and rocking no boats. It is a sad and senseless situation. If religious life declines during this period of history, it will not be because the younger generation did not appreciate its value. This younger generation exhausts itself with great causes and deep questions. No, it won't be this generation whose commitment is in question. It will be because our generation let religious life go to powder long ago by trading commitment for conformity, by worshipping at the shrine of professionalism rather than prophetism, by keeping the peace instead of raising a prophet's alarm and by guarding ourselves against death by choosing to die in place – clean, safe and proper.

Gluttony grips the world around us like a giant vise. The things we own define us and measure us and mark us socially. Those who are not engorged want to be. Those who are engorged automatically assume that they have a right to the fruits of the earth in a profusion far beyond the bounds of real need. Religious, too, who once took having the worst for granted have now learned, like everyone else of their social class and professional background, to take having the best for granted. Whatever the scriptural admonition, we too store up grain in barns. Just like everybody else. We turn our worlds in for new ones on a regular basis. Just like everybody else. We develop "rainy day" philosophies. Just like everybody else around us. We hoard resources and save money and "protect" our properties and privatize our facilities. Just like everybody else. The mind-set is a subtle one, even a funny one if it were not so contrary to everything we say we are. Products of our own society, we too often call our own engorging, our own amassings, our own security-consciousness "prudence" and "good business" and "stewardship." In the end, however, no matter how we justify it, engorgement implies at least unconscious claim to a specious birthright of unconscionable proportions. Taking more than we need of anything steals from the earth and the rest of its peoples not only their basic resources but also their human soul.

Point: In religious life, as well as everywhere else in the Western world, enoughness has too often ceased to be a virtue. Engorgement has taken its place. Whatever the vow of poverty as previously practiced did for us, it did not make us comfortable with being poor.

For the Sake of the Poor

What religious life needs now, if vows are to be worth anything at all, is a fresh and challenging call to a new understanding of poverty, one that engages this entire generation of religious in the process of living poverty for the sake of the poor. The old formation manuals, the dusty documents from another age, the constitutions and customs books that made poverty a thing of ownership rituals and the theological airy-fairy must be rooted out of our spiritual language, removed from our bookshelves and rewritten by our lives. It is precisely these materials which, ironically enough, gave us the right not to be poor and the reason to go on being rich. No matter what the old treatises say or past novice mistresses taught, religious life does not require us to control our desires to own and have and use the resources of the earth simply because "Jesus was poor." Religious must be first to reduce their wants and restrain their desires because it is a lie to say that we can possibly follow the Jesus who loved "these little ones" enough to challenge synagogue and state on their behalf and do nothing ourselves about the fact that the poor are poor. Surely the vow of poverty is not so simplistic a thing as being secure but not saturated. Vows must be made of sterner stuff than that. In our day at least, when the poorest people on earth watch on television while the richest people on earth feed their animals better food than the poor can feed their children, poverty most certainly obliges us to commit ourselves to the just distribution of the goods of the earth. By modeling that distribution ourselves and working our lives out to obtain it for others, we make the vow of poverty more than a canonical nicety, we make it real.

A vow of poverty has nothing to do, however, with institutional destitution. To talk in those terms is to fly in the face of other concerns, equally just, equally important – the care of the elderly, the education of the young, the obligation to creditors, the needs of ministry. A community that itself is destitute is in no condition to help anyone else. If anything, we need communities who steward their resources in order to be able to use them in behalf of the disadvantaged. In fact, if the world needs anything at all, it needs people who are not poor to care more than our present legislation and economic policies and trade practices indicate that the country does now about the fact that other people are desperately poor as a result of them.

The problem is not that some people are rich; the problem is that so many people are so poor. Consequently, a vow of poverty that concentrates on counting the number of blouses in the cupboard of the individual religious reduces religious life to the ingenuous and the spurious. Religious poverty is not an exercise in the arbitrary designation of personal possessions, most of which are basic at best. No, religious poverty requires a great deal more than the rationing of professional equipment for professional people. Religious poverty demands that religious as a group use their considerable resources in the service of the poor. What we do with our resources as congregations is a great deal more important than what we do to determine the number of books or blouses or shoes being used by the religious next to us. When religious reduce poverty to the personal and legalistic level, poverty has long since ceased to be real in that congregation.

Real religious poverty takes poverty seriously, not trivially, and comes down consistently on the side of the poor, sees life always from the perspective of the poor and then uses all its fine degrees, its great institutions, its highly-polished conference rooms, its manicured lawns and its favorite monastery properties to care for the poor, to speak for the poor, to shelter the poor and to influence the rich on behalf of the poor.

An authentic spirituality of poverty in a period of massive human want rests on a tripod of virtues: public advocacy, congregational deprivatization, and personal conversion. And perhaps in that order.

Public advocacy on behalf of the poor arises out of a renewed awareness of the public dimension of Jesus' own work. To say we follow Jesus, and say nothing to the affluent about their role in resolving indigence – to heal no lepers, raise no dead, multiply no loaves – cuts religious life adrift from the gospel and sets it astray. To say we know the gospels but do not know the effect of pending public legislation on the lives of the poor makes it very difficult to believe that the gospels have touched us at all.

"The poor you have always with you," Jesus said, "but me you do not always have with you." A first reading of that pronouncement seems to indicate that in the face of the presence of Jesus we may forget the cry of the poor, that it is possible to take time off from the concerns of the poor, that there are things more important than a concern for the poor. But there is another interpretation much more in concert with the rest of the Gospel message. The fact is that unless we stay constantly fixed on the teachings of Jesus, we will forget the reason for which we exist. We will never be able to really understand the continual demands which the presence of the poor makes on the life of a serious follower of Jesus. Paying attention to the scriptures is what leads us to the poor. Paying attention to the poor is what enables us to understand the scriptures. We cannot have one without the other.

Deprivatization of Religious Property

Deprivatization of religious property is key to the vow of poverty. In the years immediately following Vatican II, with its impetus to religious renewal, there was a great deal of talk about divestment, the relinquishing of property by religious communities, as essential to an authentic rendering of the vow of poverty in our time. It did not take long, however, to realize that divestment was no guarantee that religious life would be more authentic, or that by relinquishing properties religious would automatically shift the distribution of the goods of the world in the favor of the poor. In the first place, communities could only surrender so much property and still be able to house themselves without having to become wards of the state. More than that, there was still the reality that simply because religious gave up property there was no guarantee that anything more than a new service station or another

"Abbey Restaurant" would be added to the world because of it. There was, it began to dawn, a more rigorous concept to be dealt with instead: real poverty does not lie so much in what religious own as it does in what religious do with what they own. Using what we have for ourselves alone is the real sin against religious poverty. Therein lies the test.

Century after century, when religious life has declined, decline has come as a result of the social isolation of religious congregations. The further religious got from the poor, the wider the gap between the religious and the people, the more privatized religious life became, the less meaningful, authentic, effective, illuminating the life became. Religious became institutions unto themselves – staid, elite, privileged, and private. Very, very private. And that is at best theologically suspect. Why? Because everything religious own belongs to the poor. Why? Because we profess to own nothing. Why? Because all of our resources we simply steward for the works of God, we say. For religious congregations, therefore, to own massive amounts of property and then bar the poor from the door in the interests of "privacy" and "cloister" and "personal space" and "the spiritual life" makes a mockery of the vow of poverty and stewards nothing for no one but ourselves.

"Once upon a time," the Sufi write, "a thief broke into the holy elder's little prayer hut and took his only two possessions in the world: the holy book and its reading stand." "Poor man," the Sufi said, "If only I could also have given him the moon." Point: whatever we give to the poor is never enough. What we own, we own in trust for the poor, is to be used on their behalf, and takes silent measure of what kind of things it is in life that we really value. Even a cursory examination of a congregation's financial report – that assessed evaluation of what a group really does with its money, its facilities and its property – demonstrates its understanding of the vow of poverty, its real theology of religious life. No theological language appears on a congregation's financial report to obscure the effect of a group's actual life choices and make its slippage more palatable – just numbers, clear and damning numbers.

The religious congregation that forgets its mission to poverty becomes really poor of soul. Turned in upon itself, it dies because it has no reason to live other than to preserve its privacy, safeguard its institutions, insure its comfort and secure its pension fund. That kind of religious life ceases to be religious at all. Then all the symbolic gestures in the world become more theater than sign.

Personal conversion, once the primary object of the religious vow of poverty, becomes in this new spirituality the seedbed of religious poverty, the point at which we see it break out in the individual life and become possible to the Christian community that is the congregation. Without personal conversion to the meaning of religious poverty in a world now desperately, obscenely poor, poverty remains nameless, depersonalized, pure religious myth.

The notions of "detachment," permissions, and pennilessness defined the character of pre-Vatican II understanding of religious poverty. Practices of this nature conspired to create dependence, perhaps, but not identity or solidarity with those real poor who had nothing to be detached from, no personal articles to get permission for, no place to send the bills for which they had no pocket money to pay. The vow itself, shrunken to the level of the trivial, demands more serious subject matter than that, if for no other reason than that it is a vow. A lifelong, morally laden vow. The vowed life must be worth something beyond a concentration on the spiritual asceticism of the self, no matter how good-willed.

"The poverty of our century," John Berger wrote, "is unlike that of any other. It is not, as poverty was before, the result of natural scarcity, but of a set of priorities imposed upon the rest of the world by the rich. Consequently, the modern poor are not pitied . . . but written off as trash. The twentieth-century consumer economy has produced the first culture for which a beggar is a reminder of nothing." That is the role of religious life: not simply to control their own personal wants but to remind the rest of the world of the immorality of poverty; by pointing at it, dancing wildly around it; shouting, shouting, shouting "Look, look!" and never, ever failing to point out as well the practices and policies that account for it until someone, someday finally stops them.

If religious life lasts it will be because of the poor who will re-evangelize it – break open to religious the Gospel, teach them how little a person really needs to live, show them the beauties of life in the midst of its degradations. If the poor survive the brutality of the present global policies ranged against them, it will be because they saw hope and hung on tenaciously to life, heard a voice on their behalf and took hope again, awakened once more to a kind and merciful God who works through people. God willing, if religious life is to be as authentic in this period as in the last, at least some few of those people most conscious and conscientisizing of the poor will be religious again.

11.

A Call to Love

Henry Ward Beecher wrote once, "I never knew how to worship until I knew how to love." Perhaps there is no truer insight into the relationship between chastity and religious life than that single intuition. The point is a good one. If we do not love people whom we can see, as the proverb teaches, how can we possibly love God whom we cannot? At the same time, the understanding of chastity as a social concept has come across time to be so stunted, so warped that the presentation of it has been consistently antagonistic to life and growth and relationships. We have become far more conscious of what chastity denied us than of what chastity enabled in us, demanded of us, provided for us. As a result, we need to rethink the vow completely if the contemporary spirituality of religious life is to speak either to the society around us or to religious themselves.

If chastity requires the repression of sex for its own sake, the world does not need it. Repression simply masks volcanoes waiting to happen. If what stirs unbidden within us is enemy, is danger, then we are at war with ourselves for no good reason at all. And someday, somehow, it will erupt in the most destructive of ways. If, on the other hand, what we feel inside ourselves magnetizes us toward the human race, becomes the glue that binds the world together, the surge that makes us capable of thinking of someone else besides ourselves for a change, then this impulsion we have been given is gift to be nurtured, lesson to be listened to with confidence. Chastity, in that case, compels us to think about love unleashed.

There are some givens to be faced before we can rethink chastity and its role in religious life: First, lovelessness is not a virtue. Second, exploitation is not love. Third, the function of religious vows lies in more than negation of the human condition and discipline of the self. Fourth, chastity is not developmentally destructive. And, lastly, sexuality gives positive energy, and sex is beautiful.

The problem arises in the fact that those concepts exist side by side and hopelessly tangled in contemporary society. Chastity has too often become a synonym for lovelessness. Exploitation, even in marriage, has become the norm. Religious vows have been couched in terms of loss rather than gain. Self-control has been abandoned in favor of license. Sexuality has been used against women, and sex has been presented as bad, as dirty, as shameful, as something never to be done or always to be done. Chastity has come to be seen as just one more way for men to control women or the neurotic nonsense of naturally frigid people. G.K. Chesterton says it all much better, says it with holy insight: "Chastity does not mean abstention from sexual wrong," Chesterton writes. "It means something flaming, like Joan of Arc."

If the chastity of vowed religious is to have any meaning at all in a world where rape and sex, promiscuity and commitment, surfeit and human deprivation, sexism and liberation range side by side, competing for attention, making demands on the human spirit, draining the human soul, something more flaming than sterile abstinence is going to have to come from it.

The social context of chastity becomes more and more fluid every day. The rhythm method of birth control, the natural family planning programs, the chemical abortifa-

cients, the birth control pills – however we evaluate any or all
of the ways used to avoid conception – now give people control
of a natural behavior where control never before existed. The
theology of chastity – that physical abstinence is somehow more
spiritual, more sanctifying, than sexual behavior – grows more
and more suspect every day in a world of lay saints for whom
marriage supports rather than limits a couple's involvement
in, for instance, the peace movement, the ecology movement,
the feminist movement, the struggles of the world and the
ministries of the church. As a result of both scientific and
theological developments, perhaps, the context for discussing
sex and sexuality, marriage and celibacy, chastity and love has
never before been more meaningful.

For the first time in human history, sex can be more
than a taboo designed to save the world a passle of unwanted
pregnancies. For the first time in church history, sex can be
seen for what it is – and for what it is not. For the first time
in religious life, the vow of chastity can be evaluated from the
point of view of opportunity rather than denial, from an
awareness of what it permits a person to become instead of
from the point of view of what it forbids a person to do. It is
a new moment in religious history as well as in social history.
It calls for the integration of body and soul rather than a
division between the two. It is a moment worth grappling
with, an exciting moment, a moment full of possibility.

Much to the chagrin of the generation before this one,
and thanks to the new technology of sex, the 20th century
regards sexual behavior with much more freedom, much
more nonchalance than centuries before it did. On what
grounds, then, does a vow of chastity appeal today? On what
merits does it rest? For what purpose does it exist? To what
degree is it absolute? What, if anything, is its gift?

One thing for sure: whatever its standard justifications,
the traditional ideas about sex and sexuality, about the vow
of chastity and religious life, simply do not work anymore.

Gone, for instance, is the notion of the higher vocation where virgins inhabit a semi-spiritual realm released from the burden of their bodies and fitted thereby to fly with angels.

Gone, too, is an idea of perfection rooted in sexual inviolability, as if sex itself destroyed the moral integrity of the person any more than injustice and violence and greed do.

"Perfectibility"

Gone, as well, is the very notion that "perfectibility" admits of either definition or possibility in the human condition. What, after all, is "perfection" and have we ever seen it? Was Jacob perfect? Was Jeremiah perfect? Was Augustine perfect? Was Teresa of Avila perfect? Was Jesus perfect when he broke Jewish laws, got angry in the temple, walked out on the crowds in Galilee? Then, how shall the stressed and simple people that we know ourselves to be ever manage to be perfect according to definitions that defy human responses and deny the role of growth in the development of human maturity? Perfection, in those terms, is the unattainable aspiration to be what we aren't. And maybe an attempt as well to be what we should never be if human life with all its learnings is really to be human.

Finally, gone is the notion of virginity as some kind of red badge of courage to be taken into marriage to prove a woman's worth, to assure her value, to legitimate his heirs. Better yet, gone is the idea that asexuality taken to the grave is a sign of human flawlessness, of total gift of human life to God, as if the struggle to give the gift is not gift itself and a lifelong commitment to a lifestyle of contemplative service is not more valuable than simply being able to maintain a checklist called chastity.

So cataclysmic are the changes in social attitudes and insights into the sexual nature of human beings that what never was expected of men is now equally assumed to be true of the nature of women. Neither Aquinas' notion that "women do not have the strength of mind to resist concupiscence" nor Freud's conclusion that women are by nature frigid satisfies the stereotypes of either women or men. In this new kind of cultural environment, women define themselves more as adults entitled to make choices for themselves and less as objects to be used, abused and manipulated. The world finds itself, as a result, with an entirely new set of questions about the nature of sex, the meaning of sexuality – both male and female – and the place of sexual expression in society.

Sexuality has emerged as the question that simply will not go away. In this climate, sexual behavior takes on less the notion of restriction and more the idea of choice, more the idea of self-giving and less the idea of danger, more a process of human growth and less a matter of failure, more an equally human arena than exclusively a male one. As a result, everything that was once judged settled now surfaces in a maelstrom of uncertainties. It is a very scary time. For people who want answers instead of questions, the time takes on the character of spiritual chaos.

The Idea of Virginity

For religious, the question is even more fraught with a new kind of tension. What happens to the idea of virginity in a culture where people come to a religious congregation long after their virginity is long gone? The answer, of course, is that chastity is a great deal more than some sort of physical inviolability, some sort of physical prohibition, some kind of control, some kind of absence. That kind of chastity reeks of the static, the empty, the arid, the biological alone. Chastity that adds something to life rather than rejects it, on the other hand, fairly bristles with growth. It confronts a person with such deep questions and such rich experiences that to embrace it brings with it no other option than growth.

The dilemma may well be that sex has gotten completely out of proportion by being held too tightly at bay. Marriage romanticizes it; religious life denies it. The subject of the vow of chastity, then, becomes sex instead of sexuality, possessiveness instead of love, the spiritual divorced from the material, the glorification of the afterlife instead of the appreciation of life lived fully here and now, body and soul.

As a result of that kind of thinking over the centuries, all sorts of shallowness entered into the keeping of the vow of chastity. Religious life became an exercise in disembodiment, in the spirituality of the neuter, in distance, in safety, in fear. Religious rules and church canons specified, long after social norms of the same ilk had disappeared, that women could not be out in public without female companions. The dress of religious, drawn from medieval patterns and never updated, covered the entire body. No flesh was exposed, no hair showed, no body powders or scented soaps were permitted. Physical contact, even with babies, flowers, and animals ranked in some of the spiritual manuals as forbidden activities. Flowers roused the senses; babies threatened the vocation; animals, they worried, would make the unspeakable public and human comfort common. To this day, they tell us, female animals are forbidden on Mount Athos, the Orthodox monastery in Greece, for fear the natural activities of the animal population might incite sexual responses in the monks there.

In such a climate, personal interaction rated low on the ladder of spiritual development. Community friendships amounted to casual contact during group gatherings. Religious didn't swim or dance or sit in the sun or do anything that soothed the body. High back chairs and wooden benches and thick black hose took the place of overstuffed furniture, chaise lounges, or casual wear. The environment, barren of creature comforts, reeked of the formal, the stripped down, the empty. The body – never to be catered to, always to be disciplined, never to be seen – became the nemesis, the rival, the barrier to the spiritual life. Fear reigned. Sensuality lurked everywhere, sex threatened everywhere and human contact – gentle, intimate and real – was everywhere to be renounced.

For religious life, the effects of that kind of theology spelled disaster. Life existed to be negated. Isolation and loneliness became signs of holiness. Work compensated for involvement with people. Community life became a matter of strangers learning to live alone together.

Total Self-Giving

The litany of denials is devastating not because it happened so much as because it completely missed the point. Chastity is surely about total self-giving to the spiritual life, surely about our not giving ourselves over to a lifestyle of unrestrained sexual sensuality, surely about self-control, surely about self-knowledge, surely about contemplative concentration on the mystical dimensions of life. But chastity that makes love impossible, makes friendship impossible, makes privacy suspect and personal feelings unacceptable defies the very purpose of chastity. Chastity is not about not loving. Chastity is about learning to love well, to love grandly, to love with sweeping gestures. It provides an adventure into the self for the sake of others that gives new dimension to life, breadth to its relationships, freedom to the soul and availability to its demands. Sex excites but chastity enlivens living every bit as much as it equips us for the spiritual life.

"The passions are like fire, useful in a thousand ways and dangerous only in one, through their excess," Christina Bovee wrote. That kind of wisdom shakes the foundations upon which a shallow life rests. Life without passion is a sorry thing indeed.

To go through the motions of life without caring deeply for anyone else robs the religious of the very motives that inspire us to lay down our lives in the first place. There must be something worth living for that is greater than ourselves. Chastity, ironically, bridges the distance between the self and the rest of the world by broadening the scope of activity, not by restricting it. Chastity makes the bridge to multiple others possible.

By opening us to love wherever we find it, wherever it finds us, chastity puts the religious in the position of being the one person who bothers to see what others with more focused eyes may not. The passionate religious falls in love with soup kitchen people, and dirty kids, and grieving widows, and dying AIDS patients and dull and dour veterans of life who have been loved so little they themselves love not at all.

More than that, perhaps, the religious promises to love people freely so that what they love they can set free. The religious loves without binding people to herself. Chastity is love given with an open hand. The effects can be astounding.

Because they have been loved freely and without expectation, children can learn to trust, adolescents can learn to be independent, adults themselves can learn to love others without having to hold them captive. Real chastity expects nothing in return from anyone. It is simply love poured out, pressed down and overflowing. Passionate it is; clinging it isn't.

Religious life, any life, without emotion borders on the brink of the dangerous. It is dangerous to have someone sitting in front of a nuclear console who has no feeling about pressing the button. It is dangerous to have church ministers who administer the sacraments without ever noticing the people who are supposed to be being nourished by them. It is dangerous to have counselors who have not themselves felt pain or known the chasm of loss or gone wild with a sense of joy and relief. It is dangerous to form people who are supposed to be passionate mystics into passionless robots. Religious life does not need and cannot profit from religious zombies. A chastity that turns spiritual people into cement makes the spiritual life a tomb, not an invitation to resurrection at all.

But the passion that chastity enables a religious to shower on other people measures only half its bounty. The ability to express emotion is gift. Cut it off, throttle it at the source, trap it and it traps the person totally. Release it and the soul flies free. To suppress one emotion, in other words, is to suppress them all. Those who never know love will never know joy either. Those who have never known pain can never go to the heights of happiness as well. Those who have stifled their own feelings cannot recognize, let alone release, the feelings of others. Chastity is not meant to stamp out the emotions. On the contrary. It is meant to direct them in ways that are magnanimous, in ways that are true, in ways that are freeing, in ways that are life-giving.

Emotions provide the fuel that guide us through life. Deprive people of their emotions and we deprive them of energy and direction. Congregations that damp the emotions in the name of religious formation inhibit the spirit of the congregation itself, which is bad enough. But in its place, too often, depression reigns instead. The house becomes heavy with efficiency rather than effectiveness. Schedules begin to dominate human needs. It becomes more important to eat on time than to welcome the guest at the door, more imperative to pray than to answer the telephone, more important to be in bed early than to sit with people in their pain, celebrate with their joy, listen to their stories. People come and go and are never noticed for the gift they have to bring and the spiritual mildew that they dissipate.

What we do not learn to love we can never learn to live for. Then, eventually, the life dries up and leaves us wanting. Then, all the poverty and obedience that we say we vow becomes more an enshrinement of canons than a commitment to the dynamic, energizing, loving eucharistic life. Then self-knowledge evaporates, support fails us when we need it most, life drains out of us and we have no hard-won wisdom, no loving strength, no heart to give another.

Oddly enough, perhaps, real chastity provides the glue that enables relationships to develop rather than discourages them. When we love freely, we are free to love many people at once, bringing all of them into a network of friendship that strengthens us all because we have one another, we are not isolated anymore, we are saved from the disaster that is selfishness. Freed from the need to possess, to control, to own, to absorb, we are free to see goodness anywhere and, pausing to appreciate it along the way, to love it to new life, one at a time, one after another. The chaste lover loves totally for the sake of the other and, surprised by beauty, finds life richer for themselves as well.

Sexual love, glorious for its ecstasy, teaches a person the beauty of the body and the sublimity of the self. Chaste love, glorious for its commonplace attentiveness, teaches a person the beauty of the loving soul and the fulfillment that comes with the transcendence of the self for the sake of another. To teach chastity and not to teach love is tantamount to teaching spiritual exercises without teaching God. It is a purely mechanical process that leads nowhere for no reason.

The Combination of Chastity and Love

The combination of chastity and love borders on the dangerous, of course, for those who consider growth dangerous. The spiritual discipline of choice in the formation of chastity up to this period of religious life has largely been to cage people in systems of their unconscious choosing that made love impossible and then call that chastity. The trick seemed to be to tether a person until the hormones died out and then to release them to their desiccated selves no wiser for the wear. There are, as a matter of fact, two risks where chastity is concerned. One risk lies in the development of relationships and the corresponding growth they demand. The alternate risk is the kind of superficiality and spiritual infancy that comes with going through life physically "chaste" and emotionally untouched. The trick lies, not in choosing not to love, but in coming wholeheartedly to choose between the two situations so that our love is real and our chastity is fruitful.

To provide an arena where adult religious can both function publicly and grow privately means to risk the pain of exploration, the natural moments of struggle and choice, that make for wholeness, for commitment informed by information. The male church, distant from creation, from the explosion of the body into the beauty of life, emphasizes the negation of the body, the loss of the self, the concentration on the "spiritual" – as if the body itself were not spiritual. Women, on the other hand, bring to the church the gift of thinking with their feelings, of trusting human emotion, of preferring controlled intimacy to acerbic detachment. It may indeed be a more feminine approach to chastity that the world needs today, a way of learning from one another, a means of finding our deepest selves in our most personal moments. We may need to stop fearing the body long enough to find out what chastity says to the soul about love, about self, about sacrifice and about growth.

The fact is that we have always known that obedience matured from conformity to choice. The fact is that we have always understood that poverty matured from greed to generosity. Chastity, on the other hand, we have considered an event rather than a process. We imposed it from the moment of birth, all physical changes and chemical explosions notwithstanding. Perhaps, ironically, Tertullian, that great scorner of the human body was the only one who, down deep, really understood it at all. "No one can be a virgin until they're fifty," Tertullian taught. And Tertullian may well have been correct. Perhaps it is only after the body quiets, after exploration and excitement, tamed by consistent struggle and tested by life, have given way to self-knowledge and spiritual depth that we can come to the chastity that is more love than denial. When we realize that the conscious, constant recommitment to control our restless bodies is meant simply to bring us to that chastity of mind where the love of life and the love of God come together, then chastity conquers and becomes love.

It is a long and arduous road, this journey to self-control, self-giving, self-seeing. It teeters between natural exploration, emotional growth, human expression and the temptation to unconscionable exploitations. But no one walks through life whole who does not go down this road. Here lies awareness, humility, dependence on God, trust, love and faith. The way, if it is to be really holy, really enlivening, really life-giving, must be strewn more with the conviction that chastity is worth it than it is with warping guilt or senseless shame over lessons learned and loves gone headlong. It is human to be human. It is inhuman to be a plasticized person who seeks self-gratification and abandons self-control, exploits people emotionally, uses people physically and ignores the needs of the heart for the sake of the urges of the body.

Religious now move outside of cages and beyond schedules, between sexes and between sites, in ways that are common and in ways that are perilous. In this world, there is a great deal of love to get and a great deal more that must be given, a great deal that is false and even more that is true. To fall and fail along the way is no disgrace. It is, in fact, part of the process of learning to love. To become trapped in ourselves along the way, however, to give up the struggle, to become bogged down in self-satisfaction rather than selflessness, is to be true neither to the quest nor to the persons whom our lives are meant to touch. That, surely, is the greatest unchastity of all.

12.

The Call to Choose

The very idea of professing obedience in a culture that thrives on individualism and commits itself to personal freedom approaches the heights of the inimical to the Western mind. At the same time, however, it is far more than liberal philosophy that drives what is seen by many as this culture's flirtation with anarchy. The truth is that a student of the 20th century stands in the wake of actual demonstrations of the perils of obedience: The Inquisition of Christians, the burnings of "witches," the Holocaust of Jews, the apartheid of blacks, the military mass rapings of women, the burying of enemy soldiers alive, the terrorism unleashed by religious zeal, and the threat of nuclearism on a vulnerable planet. Every one of those things may have been motivated by high- mindedness, perhaps, but they were all equally corrupted, equally inflicted as much by obedience as by authority. Obedient people marched to every drum, obedient people saluted every flag, "followed every order," endorsed every tyrannical idea uncritically, and good and docile people wreaked, in every instance, untold evil in the interest of obedience. Indeed, obedience more than authority sobers Western culture and leaves it bereft of integrity. Indeed, obedience generates the deepest of cautions in the greatest of thinkers. Obedience, it becomes plain, is not always virtue.

Obedience, in fact, requires suspicion. "All religions," Alexander Herzen wrote, "have based morality on obedience, that is to say, on voluntary slavery. That is why they have always been more pernicious than any political organization. For the latter makes use of violence, the former – of the corruption of the will." If, in the light of history, we are going to make a moral contribution to the 21st century, "obedience" as we have known it must make skeptics of us all.

The moral struggle lies in the fact that not all obedience is obedience at its best. Some obedience rests in compliance, some in politics, and some in patriarchy. Only some obedience has its roots in scripture. Discerning one form of obedience from the other makes for the moral mastery of life. On it resides the function of religious life, as well. To take a vow of obedience in a world where obedience goes so regularly wrong makes the vow itself suspect. Is religious commitment a synonym for religious immaturity?

The basic question, of course, is whether religious obedience is meant to control or to free a person. Do not underestimate the importance of the question. The answer makes all the difference to the integrity of the vow itself.

A religious vows obedience, not perpetual childhood, not dependence, not mindlessness. Distinguishing one from the other makes the difference between living a religious life and being a religious robot.

If control is what obedience is about, the system soars to the height of the trivial. The truth is that it is simple to control children. The only thing necessary to assure the control of one person by another is for authority to be able to muster the force it takes to match its threats. To equate the vow of obedience with the promise to live a managed life doing petty, impossible or even personally destructive things makes a farce of its meaning. Obedience cannot be reduced to a field exercise of increasingly higher hurdles.

But if it is easy to control a person, it is even easier to remain a perpetual child whose security depends on being controlled. The only thing required to be a perpetual child is to refuse to grow up, to refuse to take responsibility for the self, to refuse to become a responsible part of the human race, a moral agent in the spending of the self. In that case, obedience saves us from ourselves, relieves us of the human condition, requires of us only enough endurance to withstand our attendant irritations with a basically repressive system. In this schema, perpetual adolescence becomes virtue. The price we pay for a guarantee of direction, for the assurance that we will not be held accountable for our own choices throughout life, is adulthood. The payoff we get is security. "Keep the Rule and the Rule will keep you," my novice mistress said. The message was clear: Religious life was some kind of moral arrangement. Turn over your life to the system here and the system would provide eternal life somewhere else. To be part of the process, all a person had to do was to take orders. Easy: time to strike a bargain.

If any people on earth know the truth of both situations – of obedience as control and obedience as liberation – it must surely be religious. On the one hand, religious life flowered in the shadow of the martyrs who knew no law and lived no law but the highest, people who therefore were the most liberated of all. On the other hand, religious life sanctified the aberration of permanent infantilism and called it Holy Obedience and became the most controlling system of all. How could anyone close their eyes to the chasm of difference between the two points of view, between one that made immaturity unacceptable and another that made adult decision-making suspect?

The arguments for control became commonplace, its scenario undignified at best. The notion of dependence on God became institutionalized as dependence on those who "stood in the place of God for us." The pecking order between

God and the governed, an embellishment of the Aristotelian notion of hierarchy, grew plainer in every age: bishops and priests first, of course; superiors or their delegates next; then the rest of humankind responsible to everyone above them, all of whom we were told enjoyed direct participation in the Will of God. The logic appalled, but the logic bewitched as well. This philosophy of the Divine Right of Kings stayed alive and well in religious life, all modern democratic thinking to the contrary, centuries beyond its rejection elsewhere. Authority, the theory taught, came from God who passed it down to the Pope first, then to kings through the Pope and finally to all lesser overlords through them. Couched in god-language and clothed in the unassailability of medieval theology, the system took on an aura of the timeless, the mystical.

Ex Officio Infallibility

The theory of *ex officio* infallibility remains seductive to this day. The practice of it, on the other hand, belies it. The theory says that without order, societies crumble. It argues that human order comes from God and resides chiefly in those in official positions. The problem is that the practice often concentrates a dangerous amount of power at the top of every pyramid in the most inhuman of ways. More than that, it diminishes respect for the personal responsibility, the personal authority, of those arrayed at the bottom of the pyramid. It is precisely the people at the bottom of the pyramid, even where pyramids rather than circles become the model of social relationships, who are intended to make sure that society does not get ground to powder at the hands of the unscrupulous, the inept or the debauched at the top. Divine-right-of-kings obedience takes what is strong and intelligent and required of every human being, institutional lackeys included – "to till the Garden and to keep it" – and turns it into servanthood. Instead of releasing all of humanity to bear responsibility for stewarding the universe, it makes some of us inherently right, unquestionably powerful, and turns the rest of humanity into moral serfs. Then a people learns to simply "take orders" and "do what they're told" and "obey authority" with never a question. Then a people can go to Nuremberg with clear consciences for the most heinous of acts. Then the *sensus fidelium* – the assent of the Christian community to the moral certainty of an official position, and the role of the Holy Spirit in the church abrades the integrity of the church itself. Obedience such as this corrupts the very concept of leadership, erodes the notion of adulthood, and corrodes the dignity of the entire human race.

In the face of compulsory public education, universal literacy and economic independence, ideas equating obedience with ethical servitude simply could not last forever. The philosophers of the Enlightenment, on the other hand, taught that authority depends on the consent of the governed. What the people at the bottom of the pyramid do not permit, in other words, cannot happen.

Clearly, an obedience based on subservience leaves us with an insipid presentation of a very potent gift, the aptitude for human responsibility. In its stead real obedience, the newly articulated thinking implies, shines brightest in the Jesus who contests with Pilate, argues with pharisees and heals paralytics on the Sabbath on behalf of higher laws.

Real obedience, the kind of obedience that makes choice imperative and questions a virtue, finds few friends in high places. This obedience spells danger both to the self and to the system. Real obedience lives on earth with one eye on the reign of God at all times. Real obedience, ironically, stands ready to serve at all times, but independent and critical of every structure that makes uncritical claim upon it.

If there is anything worrisome to those who see religious as the docile children of the church, in fact, it is the specter of a religious life full of adults. At the same time, if there is anything that might well undermine the role of religious life in contemporary society, it is psychological dependence, eternal puerility, masking as virtue.

The poles of the present-day concern about obedience mark the distance from Vatican Council I to Vatican Council II. There is simply more that religious life must be about now than vying for the sandboxes of heaven by playing obedience games on earth. The Black Box theory of obedience – that all the answers to our life questions are already designed for us by God and all we have to do to get them right is to obey those over us who know what we do not – died the death with Galileo and modern science. The fact is that we need to listen to a great deal more in life than to authority. Or, better yet, the fact is that there are a great deal more authorities in life to be listened to than merely the officers of any institution, civil or ecclesiastical. We must listen to the small, quiet voice of the Spirit within us. We must listen to life itself. We must go from answer to answer till we find a whole truth. We must learn to question and we must learn to search. Obedience is not about childish dependence, however trusting; obedience is about life gone wild with the personal awareness of personal responsibility.

Balance Between Individual and Authority

A major issue of religious life in this century is the delicate balance that must be struck between the individual and authority, both of which are universal goods. The problems that emerge from the corruption of these two are not. Individualism and authoritarianism both undermine the impact and the import of any institution. Both are to be avoided like the plague. Individualism says that the institution exists for the sole service of each of its members. Authoritarianism says that no individual has rights that are greater than the dictates of the dictator. Religious communities caught in the vise of two such competing assumptions go from chaos to coercion, torn between the two, each pole useful to no one but itself. Authoritarianism gets confused with leadership, and collegiality too often degenerates into leaderlessness. Some groups allow no individuality; some individuals accept no leadership. The result is religious life in disarray, congregations powerless to exercise their considerable weight in society and individuals with their unique gifts denied the opportunities to bring those gifts to the wider world, unhampered and unstrung.

Individuals, developed to their limits, make the charism of the group a living truth. Authority that functions to keep the charism and its contemporary implications always before the minds of the members enables the group to remain true to itself, whatever the shifts of time. Authority functions best when it brings direction and unity to a group, when it raises the questions that the group needs to face. Authority does not exist to give orders. It exists to facilitate the group's ability to facilitate itself.

When the answer of religious life to the tension between authority and individualism is a common commitment of both the leader and the members to the charism and community life of the group, the obedience of religious life to the mandates of the Gospel blazes brightly for all to see. Obedience requires both the leaders and the members of the congregation to choose, not for order, not for independence, not for control, but for whatever best advances the achievement of the gospel in this world, in every situation, at every time.

Authority is to be respected. Every institution, every life, needs guidance, needs order, needs leadership, needs a model, needs a unifying center that raises issues and honors questions. What no one needs, what no one can afford, is to annul the adult obligations of the human soul in the interests of the organization. Prostitution of the mind is not a Christian virtue.

Obedience, in other words, has been seriously trivialized in the name of religious life when what was really wanted was military submission or childish docility. The vow of obedience as it developed over time, sad to say, took a person about as far as a person could get from the Jesus who cast out demons in the Temple and confronted the authorities of the state. Then, with souls numbed to the obvious, enter the Inquisition, the Holocaust, apartheid, terrorism, Christian nuclearism and war. Enter all the demons on earth masked by someone, somewhere, as "the will of God for us."

And why does it last, this diminishment of personal responsibility in the name of honorable commitments to both state and church? Thomas á Kempis understood the dynamics of obedience best, perhaps. "It is much safer to obey than to govern," he wrote. It is much safer to comply than to confront, to conform than to challenge, to go along with the system rather than to contest it. Much safer, much surer, much easier, and in the end much more common.

And that's why obedience is a vow. Real obedience is never easy, never to be trivialized to the level of organizational order or military submission. Obedience is one thing and one thing only. It is moral choice mediated by the highest laws of God in the deepest recesses of the human heart. Anything else reeks of submission, perhaps, but not of obedience. The subject matter of obedience includes only those things that threaten the moral quality of the human soul. To protest the wanton killing of the innocent in war, to refuse to support the oppression of part of the human race, to defy governments that deny the rights of people they are bound to serve, to obstruct the destruction of the globe, to protect the defenseless from abuse, to question authorities that use their authority without regard for the people over whom they preside, this is the stuff of obedience. Anything lesser has to do with the arrangement of organizational furniture, a worthy, necessary but basically amoral task; a respect for order, perhaps, but not of the caliber of the vow of obedience.

A Mighty Weapon

Obedience shines as a mighty weapon against the oppression of the poor, the raping of the vulnerable, and the godlessness of those who seize power in order to subvert the will of God for humankind. Real obedience ranks as a truly fearsome thing.

Real obedience listens to one law and one law only, measures everything else by its standards and responds for the sake of the higher law, not for the sake of the person who pronounces it. What matters to the mind of God, what brings the world closer to the reign of God, marks the only thing worthy to be weighed in the scales of obedience. Not public success. Not private profit. Not personal piety. Not social approval. Not even the endorsement of the institution itself can bring the truly obedient to obey a lower law, a lesser lawgiver, in its stead. Nothing other than the very will of God can possibly justify the giving over of a life to the direction of others, no matter how prestigious the director.

The function of obedience does not lie in either dwarfing or manipulating the human will. Obedience, on the contrary, frees the human soul for things far greater than the petty demands of dailiness or the spiritual whimsy of arbitrary guides. Obedience frees; it does not diminish, let alone enslave a person. Human puppetry and puppeteering are not the proper subject matter of the vow. Such things simply do not constitute the breed of spiritual purpose that will inspire adults to give their lives to achieving the will of God in religious life in a period in which that kind of obedience jeopardizes the population of the globe.

At the same time, obedience neither diminishes nor exaggerates the value of personal data. What I know is only part of the knowable. My word is not the last word. But it is a word. And, though we all need to listen to every other word around it, it deserves to be heard as well or the total truth may never be known. Obeisance takes deference, exaggerated regard for the person of the authority. Genuine obedience demands considerable maturity, independence, autonomy and humility enough to risk the personal disquiet that the representation to authority of an unpopular or contrary position can take. At the same time, obedience enlarges the scope of personal experience in order to take account of the experience, wisdom and insight of others. Religious obedience is not reckless independence. Religious obedience does not obviate leadership, it demands it. The progress of a group depends on the ability of a group to face and deal with the issues that face it. It is the role of leadership to raise these, to define these, to provide the information that a group needs to deal with these. To obstruct leadership in the name of personal maturity, of higher obedience, then, is to obstruct the progress of the entire group. If anything is necessary to the development of religious life today, it is real leadership, not authoritarianism, not personal resistance masking itself as personal autonomy or "conscience." The fact is that leaders cannot lead when groups confuse autonomy with maturity.

Obedience requires us to listen to everyone so that when the winds of change blow we may hear clearly those through whom the Spirit speaks most clearly. Obedience requires us to listen to the poor and hear the ignored and bow to the little as well as to the mighty. Obedience listens to everyone and everything through the filter of scripture, the voice of God and the call of Jesus to a world in need of Eucharist, in search of Beatitudes.

In the end, then, real obedience causes the soul to soar above organizational trivia and human institutions to a state of highest humanity that knows no false restraints, abides no rules that make the reign of God impossible, honors no laws that obstruct the Spirit, bows to no one who does not bow first to the Will of God for humankind and to the governed themselves. It is an enterprise of equals in search of the Will of God, not an exercise for children intent on keeping all the parent-figures of life satisfied and happy.

When the vow of obedience functions well, conformity and compliance, rewards and systems do not take the place of God. When authority functions well, leadership means more than coercion, questions are more important than answers, giving insights is more important than taking orders. When the vow of obedience functions well, religious life emerges from the two extremes of personal license or benign dictatorship to the clear, cool certainty of mutual inspiration, of leaven, of leadership, of call.

The function of religious life is to make obedience to the highest law visible, to make human reverence visible, to make the will of God visible to all humankind, to call us all to listen to what is really calling for our highest moral response in this world.

Obedience, in other words, depends on choice. Obedience is a criteria for personal determinations, not a set of rules for living, not human implacability institutionalized. Who can possibly admire religious robots when what the world needs are religious heroes whose law is love and whose only goal is God?

Only choice makes witness real. Only choice makes growth real. Only choice makes virtue real. For religious life to be real, we must all beware of anything that makes choice suspect and maturity a sham.

What obedience needs to facilitate it, then, is leadership that makes the choices plain and the questions present and the answers possible. Only those who lack leadership fall back on authority. Only those who insist on their authority destroy all possibility of obedience and all hope for leadership. What we do not choose freely, we have not chosen at all. Force changes behavior, perhaps, but it has yet to shape a soul.

The choices we make in a world where oppression goes unchallenged, where sexism goes unnoticed, where authoritarianism goes uncontested makes religious obedience valuable. It is choice that gives us the chance to choose for God in all the daily decisions of life.

The world does not want and will not tolerate religious who stake their spiritual lives on institutional approval and define their sanctity by their inability to make a decision, to take a position, to choose for themselves between the moral, the immoral and the amoral. Obedience has been reduced to spiritual infantilism for long enough. A world in chaos needs religious now with the obstinacy of Moses and the obedience of Jesus. It is a sanctifying combination.

As Robert Frost wrote so knowingly,

> *I shall be telling this with a sigh*
> *Somewhere ages and ages hence:*
> *Two roads diverged in a wood, and I –*
> *I took the one less traveled by,*
> *And that has made all the difference.*

Religious obedience that makes no choices, makes no difference to the world at large, is not obedience at all. It is at best an exercise in childishness in a world that needs defiant saints.

13.

Light in Darkness

"The work of an intellectual," Michel Foucault wrote in his *The Concern for Truth,* "is not to mold the political will of others; it is, through the analyses that s/he does in her/his own field, to re-examine evidence and assumptions, to shake up habitual ways of working and thinking, to dissipate conventional familiarities, to re-evaluate rules and institutions." The work of the intellectual, in other words, is to confront a complacent world with the terrors which underlie its complacency. Too many systems, claiming to enhance humanity, actually exist on the backs of silent, invisible populations who are being sacrificed to maintain it. We drink good coffee, for instance, because mountain villagers die early deaths to supply it to our tables for slave wages. We demand export crops of debtor nations to such an extent that not enough lands remain to them to provide a domestic garden for starving peasants. We take food stamps from poor children and give tax breaks to the wealthy. The situation is not a new one, of course. Many a civilization has sacrificed the poor of its world on the altars of its national interests, and we have called them "pagan." Worse, they have often done it with pomp and beauty, with ritual and glory, with great clamor and deep respect. Some things with very bad aspects can look very good, if we do not look too deeply. Religious life can suffer the same fate.

For religious life to be worth its salt in this world now, we need thinkers who carry us beyond kind words and good deeds for desperate people, beyond the kind of charity that makes the obscene palatable to the kind of justice that makes the obscene impossible.

We need moral observers of the universe who will call us back to the heights of humanity from the murky depths of the kind of mad progress won at the expense of the invisible poor.

"What did they know and when did they know it?" has become a very popular political question in this period. But it is not the question that religious must ask themselves. The more important moral question for religious of this age is both more simple and more profound than the assessment of facts and memories, experiences and information. The question for religious of this time is, "What don't I know and why don't I know it?" The intellectual pursuit of the great theological, political, economic and social questions of the time is now of the essence of religious discipline in this century.

Given the interconnectedness of systems, the globalism of human life, the universalism of experience and the economics of national politics, doing "good works" may be exactly what ministers to humanity least. Without knowing it, for instance, we ourselves can become unwitting supporters of an oppressive system. We may nurse in hospitals that refuse care to the destitute, we may teach in schools that discriminate against women employees, we may invest in companies that make plutonium trigger-fingers, we may farm huge tracts of land with fertilizers that destroy that land for generations to come, we may pray prayers that enslave half the human race simply by rendering them invisible. To do anything these days without knowing who profits from it and why may undermine the very ministry to which we are most committed. No doubt about it, the intellectual life has always been important to religious commitment. Now however, intellectual development marks the merit of religious life as never before in history, if for no other reason than the scope of the issues in which we're immersed. Acid rain in the West destroys forests in the East; war in the Middle East causes depression in the West; the politics of food in the West starves children in Africa; the movement of plants from Detroit to Cambodia leaves the labor force of both regions out of work and out of hope.

To say that we can possibly minister to the poor in such a world and never read a single article on the national debt; to think that we can possibly be moral parts of a global community and never study a thing about the Third World debt; to imagine that we can save the planet and never learn a thing about ecology; to infer that we work to promote the women's issue but never go to a women's conference, read a feminist theologian or spend a minute tracing the history of ideas about women; to say we care about the homeless dying and never say a thing about the evil of homelessness or the lack of medical care for the indigent, smacks of pallid conviction at best. Simply to do kind things is not enough anymore. Professional education that fits us for particular skills but neglects to prepare a person for dealing with the great questions of human life is not enough anymore. The world needs thinkers who take thinking as a spiritual discipline. Anything else may well be denial practiced in the name of religion.

Pursuit of Intellectual Development

Pursuit of intellectual development has been a standard part of religious life in the West. Benedict of Nursia, in a Rule written in the 6th century, requires more reading and reflection time in the daily routine of monastics than he does manual labor. Life was not just prayer and work in these monasteries. Life was prayer and work, reflection and human development so that the prayer and work had substance, kept purpose, maintained its integrity. We have to know what we think before we can decide what we most need to do. We have to know why we do what we do or what we do becomes at least suspect, if not downright harmful.

On the quality of intellectual development practiced in religious life rides the ultimate effectiveness of a congregation, the depth of its spiritual life, the value of its ministries, the caliber of its members, and the prophetic dimension of its charism. For a religious to do "good works" without at the same time cultivating the intellectual gifts which enable them to pursue the problems to their causes, will surely squander the best resources a group has with which to build a flaming future.

Without great respect for learning and depth of research, religious communities move from theology to piety very quickly. Good will, good heart and great love of God find expression somehow, whether with understanding, sound development and artistry or not. It is not that piety is not good. On the contrary. All the intellectual preparation in the world will not substitute for hours of prayer and fullness of faith. It is simply that piety is not enough. Piety without theology, without study, without reflection, turns easily from the scriptural mandate to the therapeutic, to the magical, to the demonstration of the expressive without respect for spiritual consequences. More than one good idea has turned sour for lack of substance. Piety makes me feel good; theology protects me from substituting solely personal reactions for cosmic insights.

The intellectual life charts the spiritual way. Activism comes easy to religious. A longstanding history of social service, the immediate past history of organizational expansion and very personal experiences of institutional ministries won by dint of long suffering and lifetimes of hard labor, translates into constant activity, generous lives and compassionate presence to this day. The results of hundreds of years of service exist everywhere, plain to be seen: a hospital here, an old orphanage there, a fine college in the middle of the city, small grade schools in the heart of the countryside. And, more recently, peace and justice centers in old novitiate buildings, hospitality houses in the inner-city, housing for the low-income elderly on the motherhouse grounds, group gardens and soup kitchens, all testaments to the continuing commitment of religious to the suffering of the world. What is just as important to this era, however, as was the professional education of the past, is the ongoing preparation of religious in the issues of the age, and our answers to the questions, "Why are we doing what we are doing?" and "What should we be doing now?" Impulse, intuition and awareness bring fuel to thought, but they may well be short-lived without it.

The social gadflies of the system, religious must know of what they speak when they testify before Senate committees in Washington, sign petitions in rural Pennsylvania, lobby public groups about ecology, demand new legislation for the poor, discuss the ordination of women and the use of inclusive language with local clerics – and all of these in the name of God and for the sake of Christian charisms centuries old. When Benedictines talk peace, they should understand the roots of war; for a Sister of Mercy to speak effectively for women in the church, she must be articulate about the theology that oppresses them; for a Franciscan to preach on the presence of God in nature, he must be prepared to explain the ravishing damage of pollutants. Not as generals, historians or chemists, perhaps, but certainly as educated witnesses who bring to the subject not only good zeal but good thinking.

The intellectual life gives substance to the soul and credibility to the ministry. "Ideas are powerful things," Midge Dexter writes, "requiring not a studious contemplation but an action, even if it is only an inner action. Their acquisition obligates each of us in some way to change our life, even if it is only our inner life. They demand to be stood for. They dictate where we must concentrate our vision. They determine our moral and intellectual priorities." Clearly, the intellectual life is not a distraction from the real purpose of religious life. Intelligent proclamation of the caring presence of God in time is the real purpose of religious life.

A Gospel Presence

Religious are not the professional prayers of society. Religious are not this century's answer to the Mass priests of the High Middle Ages, largely illiterate men who were ordained simply to provide a stream of eucharistic liturgies in the midst of the church. Nor are religious the modern purveyors of the theology of substitution in the spirit of the medieval monastics, whose duty it was to serve their wealthy benefactors, the busy and the important people of the time, by performing their penances for them. No, religious life simply sets out to be a gospel presence in the midst of the city, whose members, steeped in prayer and compelled by contemplative courage, become voices of hope and voices of warning to the whole metropolis. To do that, a religious must be prepared as well as involved, prophetic as well as prayerful.

The moment presents a precarious situation. Plagued with anomie, faced with dwindling resources, confronted with multiple new social and ecclesial needs, struggling with the question of liturgy and language in a patriarchal church and yet, ironically, the keepers of coals still burning, still full of great life in this dying time, religious congregations must deal with the same questions as their foundresses: Is now the time to build new institutions without question or to prepare ourselves professionally for new services, without care for cost? Should we be schooling members in marine biology so that in 10 years they may be able to impact the ecology question or should we be launching mobile clinics now instead? Should we be sending younger women to universities for degrees in feminist theology or should we be renovating the retreat center in the hope of building up a new ministry to women there? Should we be studying more or praying more? The answer is yes and the answer is no. The answer is neither and the answer is both. Either approach without the other will leave religious congregations vulnerable to change or prey to the temptation of changelessness.

To retreat into some kind of meditative trance to await the millennium, to exhaust ourselves in hectic but shallow activity, to settle down simply to live out what has already died years before us is unworthy of our history, of our purpose, of our spiritual heritage and of ourselves as responsible human beings in a time of human disintegration. The fact is that none of those alternatives apply. We cannot be either one or the other. We must be both thinkers and doers, prayerful presence and prophetic witnesses.

Prophetic honesty is not an option for religious, it is a requirement. To be steeped in scripture implies that we are devoted to the coming of the reign of God. It implies, more than that, that we will give ourselves to knowing it and bringing it as well. But living out the will of God takes a great deal of study, a commitment to reflection as well as to action.

This is no time, then, for religious congregations to abandon a historical commitment to learning simply because learning is now more a spiritual discipline than a professional requirement. Just because we no longer educate in order to staff community institutions or to meet state certification requirements does not mean that we do not need education more than ever. Otherwise, how shall we ourselves know whom to follow? Otherwise, how shall we ourselves possibly know what next to do in a world full of experts in tension and in the service of so many other gods?

The intellectual life keeps alive the flame of reflection in a society more given to violent reactions and unthinking responses, short-lived in their value, too often everlasting in their harm. The world is not served by rigid conservatism, knee-jerk liberalism, bleeding-heart pleadings and bumper-sticker thinking. The religious voice must be a voice that brings to the public debate the best in tradition, the finest in theological analysis, the keenest in social perception and the most challenging of gospel values. The religious who speak for the poor must speak wisely, courageously, thoughtfully and well. We no longer have the time-tested value of old institutions to rest on for the rationale upon which we base our lives. Long gone is the age in which we all do together today what we all did yesterday because someone before us realized that it was good for another time. From now on, institution-building will be rare if for no other reason than that needs will change faster than institutions can be built to serve them. From now on, we are each going to have to weigh, evaluate, assess and determine the eternal value of every single thing we do, its relationship to charism, to human need, to eternal life and to Christian commitment. We must bring to each and every ministry more than service. We must bring the clear values and firm convictions it will take to be there as partners and advocates in the long, weary journey toward justice.

Intellectualism takes us beyond fundamentalism, above literalism to the place where people with different insights and differing needs can each come to see one another's position in ways that make the Gospel sing. Commitment is not an exercise in black or white thinking. Real commitment to a subject brings us to depths of understanding about it until there in that complexity, the virtue of love racks our souls. Then, at that point, the religious presence becomes religious.

Prayer, ministry, prophecy, community development and personal growth all demand intellectual depth. To say we live a reflective life without something of substance to reflect on makes the life a sham. "In the beginning was the Word," the Gospel teaches us. Without immersion in the Word, whatever words we say lack meaning, lack ground, lack gift. In this culture the value of education too often resides in the profit it provides. Few people study for the downright pleasure of plumbing the mind of creation but to get jobs rather than professions, that make money rather than make the world a better place for all humanity to live. In this environment, the intellectual commitment of religious to reflection, culture, beauty and truth at this new moment in history, will someday surely be seen as part of the process of *grieshog*, of burying the coals, of saving the fire, of coming to flame in new ways for a new world to see.

14.

New Perspective, Necessary Virtue

Of all the virtues touted as essential to religious life, at least one gets short shrift in history, if it is ever mentioned at all. The notion that the self is a strength to be developed rather than an enemy to be constrained looms notably absent from traditional treatises on the spiritual life. What a pity. To imagine that the spiritual life can possibly be lived to the fullest if the conduit of the self fails to mediate it in us must reflect some sort of truncated idea of what spirituality really is, some warped notion of what God really is.

The very idea that a person's spiritual life can develop to the full without ever having smelled a field full of roses or seen the lake at dawn or sat in high grass on the top of a hill or felt silk against the skin or hugged a dog or held an infant to the breast approaches the laughable. To factor out the experiences of life, the tactility of life, from the equation of holiness makes spirituality a disembodied idea. It makes the sacrament of life a very barren place indeed. It does more than make the flesh dangerous to the spiritual life, it makes it destructive of it. But the God who made all those things and every other human experience wrapped in flesh, as well, must surely be a very sensual God with a very ravishing presence. If creation proves anything at all, it must surely prove that the God who reaches out to meet a sensual creation of divine design reaches out through things, through the senses, not simply through the mind.

Mind, reason, and cognition, however – all male values – have become the ground of spiritual literature throughout the ages, not the notion of incarnation, however much they talk about it. Self has become the enemy rather than the source of the spiritual life. And therein lies the even greater pity.

The great adventure called spirituality, thanks to this approach, has been reduced across time to large doses of struggle, to the suppression of the self, rather than to an equal segment of human celebration, the recognition of the sacred in the physical as well as the spiritual self. In this system, thought and experience, the rational and the "irrational," the real and the ideal found themselves pitted against one another. Things began to be labeled and divided and ranked according to their degree of threat, their level of danger, their measure of menace to the human soul. Thanks to Greek Stoicism, with its emphasis on desirelessness during the formative days of the Church, the things that really jeopardized human happiness and moral development were whatever stirred human urgings, whatever in other words was disturbingly fleshly, doubtlessly feminine, distractingly female. Men knew that what they could not control in themselves they needed to control in others. The solution became the eternal subservience of women.

The entwining notions of spiritual purity, physical inferiority and the need to suppress female desirability put down deep and subterranean roots in the human psyche. Every century heightened the distinctions between what was spiritual in life and what was not; each generation put bigger blinders on the soul to protect it from the world around it until spirituality found itself to be more discipline than joy.

To the mind of those who considered the spiritual life a product of mind over matter rather than matter imbued with the divine, life was a minefield to be carefully trodden, not the beginning of heaven, not the bridge to the divine, not its link, its tie, its tether. For women especially, life became more and more restrictive. Women religious, whose rejection of carnal experience enabled them in the eyes of the church to transcend some of their femaleness by becoming spiritual males, more given to the "rational" elements of life, in other words, were than most other women, who were seen as fundamentally sexual beings. Asexuality, ironically enough, became the crowning measure of women held in special esteem. At the same time, they were held in special control to maintain this asexuality on the basis of spiritual premises both faulty and destructive. Women were for sex, the theologians taught, and therefore less spiritual than men. At the same time, women whose sexuality was controlled were especially valuable because they transcended the demands of their sex. The illogical logic spun both socially and spiritually out of control.

These attitudes, by and large, won the day, except among the mystics, of course, who didn't seem to have the sense to appreciate the difference between the natural and the spiritual, the fulfillment of the soul and the expression of the senses, let alone the superiority of male approaches to God over feminine insights and experience. Francis of Assisi glorified God in nature. John of the Cross tasted God every step of the way in life and talked about the ways of God with mortals through very mortal means. Julian of Norwich and Hildegard of Bingen experienced God in living color. For seers such as these, God was tangible and God loved the fleshly dimensions of life as well as its cognitive ones. For the mystics, God was more than an idea to be grasped; God was an experience to be encountered in every area of life.

To mainstream theologians and spiritual writers, though, God was an idea, Anselm of Canterbury's "that than which nothing greater could be thought," a concept beckoning us out of the world we'd been given to a self more spiritual than physical, more free of earth than formed from it.

The tenets of the system were clear: The world was divided into matter and spirit, the rational and irrational. According to the pagan philosophers from whom early Christian writers adopted the idea – rather than from the very earthy inclusiveness of Christ – male semen provided the raw material for the rational soul, the female *mens* its material form, its body. Chief among things that jeopardized the rational – the masculine, in other words – was the feminine. Sexism came full blown from the speculation of pagan thinkers about the "natural" superiority of rational men over "irrational" women and became the basis for a Christian spirituality of domination that to this day minimizes women in the name of God, trivializes the feminine, enshrines the male, institutionalizes the masculine, diminishes the Christian message and plagues the world still.

The Disjunction of the Spiritual and the Material

The disjunction of the spiritual and the material proved to be a drastic one for the whole human race. Like ants in the hands of a giant, the whole world now depends on the fiat of men whose male treatises define themselves as the crown of the human race, next to God, the "head" of the human family and beholden on this earth only to themselves. It is a sad monopoly of humanity. It is an even sadder loss of human resources and the feminine value system in a world reeling from the consequences of machomania.

And how did it happen? Easily. Men won the argument because men framed the argument, defined the terms of the argument, controlled the outcome of the argument and forbade women to discuss the argument, simply by keeping them out of the intellectual arenas and ecclesiastical courts where the conclusions from it were drawn. But men were wrong and we pay the price for it in every arena to this day.

Having categorized life into clearly separate categories – animate and inanimate, vegetable and mineral, human and inhuman, white and "colored," slave and free, masculine and feminine – they have fashioned us a globe at war with itself. "All of nature and most humans," Aristotle taught, "are created to supply the comforts and necessities of the higher class. . . . And," he concluded, "this [subordination] is good – for both the slaves and the women." Aristotle, too, like Shakespeare's Macbeth, "should have died hereafter," after he could see the damage such poor reasoning had done age after age after age. He might have wanted to write another essay. The fact is that the male hierarchy having been established, the hierarchy has ruled according to its own principles to the brink of its own ruination.

Machosim vs. Feminism

Machoism is neither good theology nor good spirituality. Machoism destroys creation and its creatures and calls the destruction good – "national security," "economic progress," "woman's role," and "God's will."

And it won't work anymore.

To maintain a spirituality of this ilk and call it religious – worse, for religious to maintain a lifestyle like this and call it spirituality – cries to heaven for vengeance. We must do better than that if religious life is to have meaning in our age at all. We must do better than that or abandon half the human race in the name of religion.

If anything marks the distinction between modernism and post-modernism, it is the emergence of a new worldview that traces the current rupture of human relationships and global security to the institutionalization of the solely masculine virtues of control, order, domination, dominion and "reason," and requires the restoration of human balance through a recognition and reverence for the feminine values and principles of life. Feminism is a worldview that revisions the world from the perspectives of the equality, humanity and dignity of every living thing. Feminism requires ecology. Feminism assumes globalism. Feminism dismantles patriarchy, hierarchy and dualism. Feminism gives Christianity the opportunity to be Christian for perhaps the first time since Jesus.

But anti-feminists are not all wrong in their fear of feminism. Feminism is indeed a hazard to the kind of system that sees the needs of the globe as secondary to the needs of the corporations, that assumes that relationships are built on natural inferiority, that fosters subservience as acceptable, that treats animals as disposable for the convenience of human beings, and human beings distinct from the chain of life that binds all of us together, one common mass of creation alive with our God. In the face of those things, feminism inspires both obstacle and answer. In response to systems like that, feminism presents both the world at large and religious life itself an unyielding challenge, a spiritual promise, an undying hope in the empowering will of God for all the globe. Feminism is not about femaleness. Feminism is about freeing all of life from the scourge of domination. When women are free, men will be free. When women gain the right to grow to the fullness of God's will for them, the globe will gain the right to be freed from the theology of domination called the theology of dominion. Feminism is about restructuring the world to make it a place where all of life, at every level, is sacred.

Feminism presents us with the major spiritual challenge of the age. Without feminism, ages to come may never come at all. We justify the destruction of too many rain forests by the theology of domination. We murder, mutilate, rape and impoverish too many women on the basis of male superiority. We have massacred too many peoples on the basis of white power. We have made a travesty of God and called God male to maintain the travesty.

What the world needs now to save itself, if it can possibly be saved at all, is a feminist spirituality that calls to conscience anything that sees the world, interprets the world, explains the world or governs the world through solely male eyes, for solely male purposes, with solely male morals, out of a solely male-defined theology. Anything. And therein lies the cross and the crown of this century's religious life.

Feminism and female are not synonyms. Many men are feminists. Some females, using all the positions, privileges and public acceptance won for them by the feminism of this century, maintain they are not. For people who grapple with the question of feminism, the problem seems to lie in the understanding of what feminism really is. For the Christian, for the religious, the source of the concept should be obvious. And with the obvious, the obligating.

To serve the world, to say the Gospel but not to unsay a philosophical system that sets itself over and against the rest of the universe and all its resources, preaches a false God. Feminism is actually a very simple concept. Feminism is a commitment to the equality, the dignity and full humanity of all human beings to such an extent that we dedicate ourselves to effecting the changes in structures and relationships that make the fullness of humanity possible for everyone. On the other hand, straightforward as it is, it requires a whole new way of seeing the world and everything in it. Feminism views the world from the point of view of the meaning of creation rather than the concentration of power. To the feminist, whatever has been created is good and gifted and necessary to the development of the human race, to be respected, to be listened to, to be included in the panoply of power that affects its existence. To the feminist, nothing is made for the "comfort and necessity" of something else, nothing is without its own dignity, its own meaning, its own value, its own needs, its own gifts, its own rights. To the feminist, life is not a matter of the survival of the fittest, it is a matter of the fullest possible development of us all. Feminism is a philosophical system that has for its subject the equality of women and, concomitantly then, the salvation of the universe because once we free the slaves we correct what has enslaved them. Feminism is a very holy, very Christian thing. Feminism follows the Jesus who raised women, considered worthless by the society around them, from the dead. Feminism follows the Jesus who sent women to proclaim his messiahship to foreigners and announce his resurrection to men. Feminism follows the Jesus who, conceived by the Holy Spirit but born of a woman, makes plain the essential role of women in the divine mystery of salvation.

How can religious life possibly be religious if it is not feminist as well?

If justice is a constitutive element of the Gospel, then equality is of its essence. It is impossible, in other words, to maintain anyone in subservience and claim to be just, claim to be Christian. But if we maintain that God built inequality right into the human race, then equality is a lie to begin with, a divine joke, a serious misinterpretation of the meaning of life. Then everybody is meant to be somebody's lackey. And what kind of Christianity, what kind of cry for the Beatitudes, is that?

To Steward the Globe

To steward the globe, we must steward its gifts. But right now the entire globe stands robbed of the gifts of women which are never brought to bear on the major question of life: famine, war, birth, economics, government, militarism or international relations. We are in a sorry state indeed, with most of the world's poor, women; most of the world's starving, women; most of the world's refugees, women; most of the world's enslaved, women. What kind of keeping of the garden is that? What kind of God are we to believe willed that?

What feminism seeks is true partnership for the care of the earth, true balance of its gifts, true integrity in its relationships. Without it we can never mend a universe distorted by force, given over to power, built on oppression and made the captive of might. Everywhere, in every system on earth.

For women religious, women of privilege, to deny the Christian claim to feminism and therefore to spirituality, to deny the self for the sake of a bloodless, and therefore Godless, spirituality is to make covenant with all the oppressors of the world. Then, the oppressed becomes the oppressor and women everywhere know that sisterhood has become a lie.

There are only four periods in the history of humankind, the anthropologist Margaret Mead is said to have taught, after which nothing on earth was ever quite the same again. And those periods are, she said, the period of Evolution, the period of the Ice Age, the period of the Industrial Revolution and the period of the Women's Movement.

Feminism is alive and awake on the globe. The Holy Spirit is moving over the waters and She is intent on a new world order built on creation, built with women as well as with men, built for the oppressed everywhere. Religious life, too, cannot, will not come through this period without being changed by it. The real spiritual question is what will religious themselves change because of it.

Religious who once provided services for women must now make cause with the very essence of feminist thought – for the sake of their own spiritual liberation, the liberation of men, and the emancipation of God from sexist and patriarchal definitions. Then we shall all be able to minister with integrity and credibility for the sake of a globe in danger from policies and theologies too long repressive of the feminine. Feminist spirituality calls for a new kind of spirituality in all of us. The rational, the ritualistic, the repressive spirituality of patriarchy that divides the world and everything in it into good and bad, high and low, living and non-living, agent and object must give way now to a spirituality that, integrated, sees God in everything, inspiriting, recognizes the Spirit in everything, inclusive, sees equal value in everyone, humble, sees no one and nothing as more or less acceptable to God, and incarnational, sees God and God's grace present everywhere in everything. Feminist spirituality is indeed dangerous for the orthodoxies that categorize and control. It demands a new ecology of life, not simply a reform of what is. It is the hope of the earth, the liberation of the oppressed, the emancipation of imagination, the very restoration of the real meaning of God.

The spiritual discipline of this time is the development of a new worldview, one based on human equality rather than on male power, a concept specious at its roots and corrupting of the spiritual life. It is a great moment for religious life. We stand to be visible signs of a world built on equality, the gifts of women, the respect for the feminine and the awareness of the feminine, as well as the masculine nature, of God. Perhaps nothing in our time calls us more to conversion, more to holiness, more to genuine spiritual insight. Perhaps nothing in our time means more to the ongoing development of the world as well as to a genuine, a holistic spiritual life.

15.

A Call to Formation

Religious life has long been at crossroads – for many of today's religious almost all their consecrated days, in fact. It has been a time of surge and failures, both personal and institutional, of unclear formation and unrelenting challenge, of new convictions and deep confusion. It has been an exciting time for religious life but it has not been an easy time.

The feelings of tension and uncertainty that exist in religious congregations to this day, however, are not, I think, because it has been what social scientists would call "a period of adjustment." On the contrary, periods of adjustment are normal in any organization and in every part of life. Periods of major social change certainly demand great energy and considerable, often continual, risk. At the same time, change usually occurs without great incident and almost always more rapidly than first imagined possible. No, the uncertainty simmering in religious congregations and communities across the land today arises, I believe, because there has been, and is yet in many cases, deep disagreement about exactly what it is in religious life that needs to be renewed if the coals are to burst into flame again in our time.

Some want things to be very like they used to be and definitely as "good" as they perceived them to be before the upheaval generated by the period of Vatican II. They want thriving institutions, stable ministries, total public approval, comfort in the church and privilege in the state. For them, that is religious life at its best; religious life as it ought to be. Others, on the contrary, want religious life to be totally unlike what it was. They want personal freedom, total independence, congregational autonomy and professional ministry without personal cost or public pressure.

The last 25 years of religious life have been a struggle of every shape and hue between the two approaches to renewal. Some groups have tried in vain to maintain or resurrect a pre-Vatican II religious life by doing more of the old and doing it better. A few of these groups exist and are functioning effectively but, by and large, the model has not swept the land. Other groups have done a renovation task of mammoth proportions. Anything and everything that looked like life before 1962 has been reshaped, painted and resold as new – new schedules, new lifestyles, new ministries in the shell of the old. Old ministries, old prayer forms, old community structures have all undergone cosmetic change – a guitar here, a committee there, a bevy of new clothes here, a pano-rama of new works there. But underneath the flurry, little or nothing has really changed, except, of course, that people who ceased to see religious life as effective before the changes now cannot recognize it at all.

The problem is that neither position – neither restructuring the past nor regilding it – really answers the situation. In fact, we have a model to warn us of the consequences of both. After the destruction of the first temple at Jerusalem in 563 BC, Israel made every attempt to rebuild the temple in the model of the first. The result was a lackluster lament for the days of past glory, a poor imitation of a great time, a superficial approach to a fundamental problem – and it did not last.

The second temple, despite its expansion under Herod, went down as easily as the first, fell again under pressure, had nothing whatsoever new to offer that could strengthen the Jewish nation in the face of new assaults and foreign challenges and then, only then, finally, did the change in the nation become fundamental. Then when the past was clearly over, the people of the place became the people of the book. Then, when the new attempt at reinstitutionalizing sacrifice proved as feeble as the past attempt, the people of sacrifice became the people of the word. Then the Jews of the desert became the Jews of the diaspora, and a national religion brought with it an international impact felt throughout the world.

Only after the destruction of the temples did the witness to Yahweh in Israel become a witness to Yahweh in the world. Driven out of where they had been and had intended to stay forever, Israel became a nation of witnesses in dispersion.

If religious life is ever going to be itself again, it is imperative for our own generation to understand that the first temple of religious life, the pre-Vatican II model, has fallen and that the second temple, our own, is shaky to the core. It is imperative to understand that we are being called to a newer, even deeper commitment than the one before now; that we are being called out of seclusion in the Catholic world into the whole house of God, out of piety and personal perfection into deep prayer and the implications of psalmic vision; out of clerical status into Christian commitment; out of the upper room where big, brave, bold apostles went into hiding and called it discipleship, back to the foot of the cross. This time, clearly, it is we ourselves who will not thrive again until we go there ourselves.

Time to Become a New People

The truth of the matter is that we cannot claim to be building the new religious life until we call for and form for the new direction. It is too late now to rebuild in the shell of the old. It is time to become a new people again. It is time to realize that the formation of renewal communities and the candidates who come to them is not a matter of instituting a plethora of insignificant changes, helpful as these may be to becoming an incarnational presence in the world. No, real renewal of religious life depends on this generation's living the new ideals and carrying the charism in radically new ways into God-awful new places.

The information is in and the information is clear. Professional studies of both religious communities and service organizations in general confirm what social psychologists have for over a generation traced in individuals caught in torrents of change: lack of role clarity at a time of institutional transition leads to the rise of anomie, of listlessness, of a sense of purposelessness in the members. "Why did I come?" people in anomie ask. Then, lacking reasons convincing enough to make the ongoing effort to stay worth their while, they become mired in institutional depression or personal despair. The effects on both the institution and the person are serious and debilitating.

Lack of role clarity leads to personal disillusionment. "Why do I stay?" they weep. People simply don't know why they are doing what they are doing. For what purpose? To what end? With what results? So why do it? Lack of role clarity leads to mediocrity, leads to the death of meaning and a darkness of heart, leads to a soul-sickness that poisons the environment and wearies the spirit, that lowers the level of laughter and erodes the glue of time, that allows me to make peace with the comfortable life and tempts me to take myself back – one deep sigh at a time.

"Only the consciousness of a purpose that is mightier than any and worthy of all," Walter Lippman wrote, "can fortify and inspirit and compose the soul." Past answers to current questions do not satisfy, old reasons for doing new things simply do not impel hearts in a world full of new problems. The past, whatever its glory, will not form the foundation for a new generation of religious because, fine as it was then, it is no reason to stay now when all the circumstances have changed. The work, the social situation and even the theology of religious life are different now. The mystique is gone; all that is left is the gospel.

When the world is starving around us, and dying in front of us, and being eaten up by military budgets and Third World debt payments, this is no time to talk about a poverty that symbolizes but secures, a chastity that isolates and an obedience that conforms. It is precisely our security that is killing us, and our isolation that is insulating us from the gospel, and our "obedience" that is making us docile attendants of oppressive and unjust systems. We have taken the very vows that were meant to free us and turned them into institutional niceties that now enslave us to the economic standards and antiseptic social strata and patriarchal systems to which we say we are counterculture.

To talk about vocations and formation and not to talk about living foolishly is to put more stock into rebuilding the temple than into living the Torah. There are for us, like the Chosen People, great issues – seven in particular – that need to be faced in this transition from temple to Torah, and face them we must or the future of religious life is already decided and already dead.

Viability

First we must face the issue of *viability:* A community is not viable simply because it tinkers with change. Too many communities changed to survive and then, when the social costs of change became apparent, they stopped changing for the same reason. They changed without theological conviction or spiritual consciousness. They changed but they did not renew the life energy, the consciousness of new purpose, needed to make the changes enlivening. Change for its own sake is frivolous. Change for the sake of personal comfort without public impact is meaningless. Only change that enables us to change the world for the sake of the gospel engages the religious soul to its real depths.

Religious congregations made numerous physical adaptations in the lifestyle of its members – a necessary component of the renewal criteria laid out in Vatican II, when it called religious to examine "the needs of the members, the spirit of the founder and the signs of the times" – but had a more difficult time, it seems, bringing to new forms the hallowed meaning of each that is essential for the changes to be seen as spiritual as well as comfortable. As a result, too many religious have missed the relationship between the virtues of the past and the virtues of the present. This life is only viable if it is worthwhile, and it is only worthwhile if members find being in it more spiritually compelling than not being in it. Without a clearly defined and demonstrated spiritual component, religious life becomes more and more questionable every day. When renewal began, older members feared the loss of the spiritual elements of the life, while younger members sensed the loss of the social impact of the life. It is time for both elements to be integrated again.

Instead, many communities went so far and no further. They changed a little physically and a little spiritually but they could not, it seems, link the two. They took off old habits but they could not put down old ministries and old states of mind. In too many instances, colleges and hospitals and academies were not closed. They simply died on the vine while the members got older every day and less able to turn their energies to new things. They did not, in other words, close dying ministries in order to launch more necessary ones. They simply watched while ministries, once vibrantly unique but now weary and routine, melted under their feet, like ice floes in the middle of the Sahara. As a result, a new generation, looking for ways to commit themselves to the new concerns of their own era saw good people doing old work, rather than risk-centered people doing the new work that needed to be done. And young people looked elsewhere for ways in which to work out their own calls to co-creation.

Consequently, it is now not a question of whether this old form will die. The old form has been dead for decades. The only question now is what do we want to be caught dead doing: the dwindling works of the past century or the fledgling works of the next? It is no longer a matter of imagination that is needed – as it was in the 60s – to redefine the role of religious in a new kind of society. No, the needs are all too clear: homelessness, ecological experimentation, hunger, peace, AIDS, globalism, the new world order, ethics, lifestyle, alternative education programs, hospitality, feminism, and the need for spirituality programs to address the dearth of spirit – even in the churches. What is needed now is the spiritual intensity to build from scratch, if necessary, however old we are, however limited we feel, the works that are needed in our time, not because they are new but because they are necessary both for the good of society around us and for our own spiritual integrity.

What formation programs are forming congregations to meet these new needs? The formation program that does not require free service to the poor, presence to the issues of the time, commitment to an understanding of liberation theology, ecumenism and feminism is not forming for viability. Religious life will be viable, worthwhile, authentic only if it does something to bring the reign of God where God's will is most missing right now. When religious life becomes a monument unto itself, it is not viable even if it goes on existing. History is certain about that, a veritable videoscape of congregations come and gone as they clung to old forms in the face of new needs.

Value of Religious Life Itself

Second, we must face the issue of the *value of religious life itself.* "Why be a religious?" people, even some religious, ask. "The laity do now what religious used to do." The question insinuates its own answer. The real question is, "Why not be a religious?" The fact is that for some people religious life points the way that best calls them to their finest and most spirit-filled selves. It is not a better way, it is not a higher way, but it is the only way for some persons to come fully alive to the will of God, in the spirit of God, for the reign of God.

Religious life promises a life steeped in the scriptures and flung against the callous or uncaring agendas of the world like a comet in the sky. Religious life raises a chorus of seekers standing in the middle of an affluence that breeds poverty and a power that breeds powerlessness, all shouting together in unison, "Enough, enough of this deprivation. Enough."

Religious life provides for a gathering of the spiritually single-minded to confront the rich, who are blinded by riches, and to support the inhumanely poor, who are in despair because of their poverty, shouting in their name, "More, these need more."

Religious life is a crosscurrent in time, showing a way where there is no way for those who, on their own, attempt the same intensely spiritual path with little to guide them, with only limited support. The function of religious life is to raise up groups whose lifestyle is so authentic, so inspiring that others can see in them that the way is possible and take courage themselves in its pursuit. By their very existence they encourage people who are trying to live that same gospel life, but alone in the world around them. Religious communities provide a harbor for people caught in the storms of life. They live in the world in such a way that the highest quality of being can never be forgotten and, standing steadfast in the midst of struggle, give heart to many.

As long as the human soul reaches out for the truth of life, for the intangible, and as long as religious stay rooted in the spiritual side of life, religious life will be worth it. For everyone, both inside and outside the group.

The formation program that does not form people in the history of spirituality, in the social role and servant status of religious life – whatever its form – in prayer and contemplation, and in spiritual reflection in a highly materialistic world, will at best reproduce a fruitless hierarchy of pseudo-shamans – if it reproduces anything at all.

The Institutional Church

Third, we must face the issue of the *institutional church*. It is important to remember that tension with the Church is a historical part of the development of religious congregations. Indeed, when religious are doing what they are supposed to do in church and society – opening new areas of ministry, raising new questions, developing new roles – tension between the keepers of the tradition and the developers of the tradition looms almost inevitable. For instance, the institutional church did not want women religious on the streets, even to feed the hungry. Ask Mother McAuley. They didn't want women to nurse, even when men were dying on the battlefields. Ask the Sisters of Charity of Nazareth, Kentucky about that. They didn't want women to teach boys, even pre-teen boys. Ask Benedicta Riepp and the Benedictines about that. And they didn't want women in male theology classes as recently as 35 years ago. Ask Sister Madeleva and the Sisters of the Holy Cross, who created the first degree program in theology for women in this very generation.

But nuns did it all anyway, whatever the resistance from the church, and they never stopped thinking of new needs – then or now – despite the threatened danger to their immortal souls for stepping over canonical traces, out of their convents and back into life. Stretching the institution is clearly a function of religious life. The documents call it "the prophetic dimension." The ecclesiastical bureaucrats often call it "disobedience." Yet, most ministries now proudly displayed in the Official Catholic Directory as "diocesan" programs – soup kitchens, peace and justice centers, hospitality houses, battered women's centers, AIDS hospices, refugee centers, spirituality centers – were all begun not by the dioceses themselves but by nuns, many of them acting independently, during the past 25 years in what is supposed to be the period of the demise of religious life. But if that is so, then there is a lot of life in this death. And these ministries were being founded while religious were being corrected for not being in schools and not wearing uniforms.

Religious are by nature, in other words, changers. So, the message is clear: The tension will surely go on if religious go on doing what must be done. It is just that tension for which we must provide formation. Programs that do not teach the historic struggle between charism and institution will never develop in the next generation of religious to come the courage it will take to preserve the charism of the order in the face of the institutions of the church. In fact, it may be precisely when we become the good children of Mother Church that we run the risk of becoming its underdeveloped children as well – loving and lovable, perhaps, but dependent and depressingly unimaginative at the same time; open to direction, yes, but closed to the Holy Spirit at the same time. In an age long past business-as-usual, we must teach again that religious are meant to be the wake-up call of the Church.

The Women's Issue

Fourth, we must face *the women's issue* and its effects on religious life. Feminism is not a political ideology based on female chauvinism. Feminism is another whole way of looking at life, for men as well as for women. It is a completely different worldview. It is a worldview that honors feminist values – equality, relationships, life, creation, nonviolence – and holds them as just as necessary to the human enterprise and the decision-making process as are masculine priorities. Feminism rejects domination of all kinds. It suspects the limitations of a theology that calls God male and calls us back to the God who is pure spirit, all Being, total life. It rebels against the rape of the earth, and the rape of the mind, and the rape of the soul and the rape of the body, even in the name of marriage and obedience, even for the sake of a tradition that is tradition because it is not in the interest of the powerful to change it.

Feminism affects the ministry, theology and spirituality of anyone – woman or man – whose consciousness is touched by it. It will not be long before both women and men will reject a religious life that does not use its considerable influence, education, and corporate power to resist the degradation of women everywhere, in both church and state.

We must form both women and men for feminism. Every novitiate in this country must teach the status of women worldwide, the theological inconsistencies that ecclesiastical chauvinism breeds, the danger to the globe of institutionalized machoism, and the loss of credibility to a church that preaches equality but does not practice it.

Of all the issues facing religious life, feminism is surely the most veiled and the most dangerous because it brings us most in conflict with the flow of history. We can, as church and congregations, all close our eyes, sink into our albs, or become the female part of a patriarchal system if we will, but if we do it will not be long before religious life will die of its own sexist disease.

New Ministries

Fifth, we must face the issue of *new ministries*. If we are earnest about this life, we must exist for the people for whom Jesus existed: the lepers, the outcasts, the women, the sinners, the living dead of life. Translate today: the homeless, the street-walkers, the poor, the invisible, the unwashed, the loud, the uncouth, the desperate. Of course, religious may walk with the rich and powerful but only if they talk there for the poor and dispossessed – as Jesus did in the rich man's house. It is not an easy thing to do. If religious communities are going to deserve to exist in the next century as they did in the last, they are going to have to pledge themselves in clear and corporate ways to the needs of the new poor. Religious communities must not only encourage individual members to develop new ministries, they must as congregations develop new forms of ministry as well.

Religious must ask themselves what they stand for as congregations and who knows it. When religious stood for education and health services and the care of indigent children, everyone knew it. When religious stood for the insertion of Catholic ministry into a civil system, no one called it political, and everyone recognized its presence. Religious congregations stood as bulwarks against ignorance, illiteracy, disease, abandonment and secularism. We turned all our resources in those directions. Now we have the best educated groups in the world, each member of which has high-level professional visibility, yet, at the same time, the congregation itself with all its potential power has become almost totally invisible. Unless and until we turn our corporate energy to the specific issues and social questions of this age, educating the world to their importance, advocating for change and modeling fresh responses ourselves, the question of why we bother to go on together is both a valid and an imperative one. Social psychologists tell us that people join groups in order to do together what they cannot possibly do alone. It is possible that we are trying to do entirely too much alone, one by one of us, instead of as a congregation itself. It is possible that having given up our institutional ministries, we have not made a successful transition to a new kind of corporate witness through the concentration of each individual ministry to a common congregational theme – poverty, women, peace, hunger, ecology, ecumenism – that most reflects the charism of the order in contemporary society.

The fact is that a congregation without a corporate commitment has nothing for which to form a person at all. Why would we take a person's life for no good reason? Religious congregations must release everywhere in society, at every level, through every individual member – wherever those members are, whatever separate things they do – the white heat of the congregation's charism on the hard, cold questions of the age in one great corporate mind and one easily seen communal heart. Otherwise, what are the charisms for in this day and age?

It is no longer a case of converting old buildings into new kinds of work. It is a case now of knowing what part of the reign of God we are in the process of creating, with or without buildings, and then each of us must be about creating it wherever we are. We must form for corporate commitment.

Spirituality

The sixth major issue of the time in religious life is the issue of *spirituality*. It is surely true that old spiritualities of negative asceticism and rigid schedules and total withdrawal and childlike docility to organizational conventions cannot possibly form the kind of spiritual adults needed to forge new ways of being where the needs are: in the barrios, on the streets, in women's shelters, in the courts, on the civic boards, in congressional hearings, with the lonely, on militarized borders, with the refugees, with the urban poor, in the newspapers and television studios that enable us to say aloud our no to oppression and our yes to the reign of God. No, privatized spirituality will not do. But great spirituality is needed nevertheless. A deep and regular prayer life is needed. The support of a spiritual community is needed as perhaps never before.

The formation program that confuses work with prayer, good intentions with the spiritual life, profession with commitment, will only hasten the collapse of a good structure brought down by the daily weight of apparent unsuccess, of the grinding fatigue of slow social change. Who knows how much of anything oppressive or evil will be changed by all the hours of work we do? But that is unimportant. What is important is only that, impelled by the gospel, imbued by the scriptures, alive with the fire of justice, sustained by prayer, we go on. Spirituality fuels the soul with the spirit that makes ongoing commitment possible.

Value Definition

The seventh issue facing religious life today is the question of *value definition*. We must begin to realize that the virtues being asked of religious today are just as sanctifying, just as ascetic, just as holy as any of the virtues asked of us by the spiritual life before this time. Religious discipline has not gone soft; religious life has gone authentic – authentically adult, authentically demanding, authentically gospel. What religious life requires of us today is an authentic response to today.

Silence, fasting, blind obedience, conformity, regular community prayer and personal invisibility – all cornerstones of the pre-Vatican II world of religious service, personal sanctification and communal asceticism – must give way now to even more developmental and often more challenging virtues. Contemplation, risk, trust, conversion, justice, love, personal responsibility, fidelity to the law above the law, depth, feminism and globalism. These are the virtues, I am convinced, that will maintain the coals, guard the fire and light the flame of a new religious life today. These. These primarily. These most of all. Privatism has had its day. The world is now too complex for a spirituality that is not wide enough for the globe, deep enough for the Mystery that pursues us all, everywhere.

Clearly, it takes grounding in the Spirit to move through darkness and not to quit. Otherwise, the long hard road ahead of us will be far too far for the going, and we will have confused achievement with commitment. Indeed, we must form our lives in prayer so that the spiritual life can overflow into life, sustain us in the deaths we are dying and carry us to new heights in hard times. "The purpose of prayer, my daughters," Teresa of Avila said over and over again, "is good works, good works, good works." Without prayer to guide us and sustain us and break open our frightened hearts, good works will not be possible in a time when one age has ended and the new one – only a ghost now, perhaps a myth – has yet to begin. Without good works, prayer falls empty on the ears of the human race.

Viability, purpose, charism, feminism, ministry and prayer are the formation acupuncture points of the age. When almost one billion people in the world are illiterate and two-thirds of the illiterate are women, how can we say we are forming religious and not form for equality? When capitalism becomes less and less humane every day in this country, how can we say we are forming religious and not form for justice? When we poison the globe to the point of extinction and religious themselves do not recycle, do not study the ecological question, how can we say we are forming religious and not form for globalism? When weapons and not wheat are the major export of the country we call the guardian of freedom, when we refuse to be a welfare state but make ourselves a warfare state and never even have the grace to blush, how can we be religious and not form for peace?

We need formation programs that enable us to serve the poor, educate the poor, empower the poor, advocate for the poor, and make the connections that unmask the pitiable lives of the poor. If the world in which we live is any measure whatsoever of the validity of our commitment to the gospel, these, then, must be the basics of religious vocation, of formation for religious life. None of them can be reduced to textbooks and the study of the congregation's constitutions. All of them must be alive in the life of the congregation itself. Then religious life will become the life of the Jesus whose temple, torn down, rose again glorified.

Religious of this age, if the decline of immediate past ministries is any signal at all, must form for a religious life that uses institutions, perhaps, but is not defined by them. We must form a people who follow the Jesus who walked from Galilee to Jerusalem touching the unclean, consorting with sinners, contending with the teachers, giving the hungry food he did not have, talking to the rich on behalf of the poor and praying on mountaintops, in synagogues, and deep in desert places on his way to cleanse a temple – not to traffic in the trivia of maintaining the superficial and empty trappings of religion at any cost.

Once upon a time, a story tells of three monks who knelt in the chapel in the dark morning before dawn.

The first thought he saw the figure of Jesus coming down from the cross and coming to rest before him in mid-air. "Finally," he said to himself, "I know what contemplation is."

The second felt himself rise out of his place in the choir. He soared over his brother monks and surveyed the timber-vaulted ceiling of the church, and then landed back in his place in the choir. "I've been blessed," he thought, "with a minor miracle, but in humility I must keep it to myself."

The third felt his knees growing sore and his legs tired. His mind wandered until it came to a stop on the image of a luscious hamburger laden with onions and pickles.

"No matter how hard I try," said the devil's helper to his master, "I can't seem to tempt the third monk."

The point is clear: False holiness betrays us. The world does not need religious who live in clouds and darkness and intent on encapsulating themselves in pseudo-spiritual bubbles. The world needs religious who, for the sake of others, live in this world well.

Single-Minded Centeredness

To seek vocations now, to form for religious life now, to create a prophetic religious life now, we must form for single-minded centeredness, not for pious perfectionism. We must form for wild caring, not for pathological individualism in the name of self-development. We must form for risk, not for social approval, not for community conformity. We must form for social critique, for blistering, searing confrontation with any system that makes the poor, poor and keeps the poor, poor; that speaks justice but practices oppression; that talks about the will of God by making itself the will of God. We must form for community-building beyond ourselves, for the shaping of a community of strangers in a global world. We must form for enoughness, not for a poverty that is based on "permissions" but never, ever knows want, and is very, very secure indeed. We must form for "locusts and honey" in a world full of business suits. We must form for voluntary marginalization, for separation from the system rather than for privilege in it. We must form for the prophetic rather than for the obedient, for the pastoral rather than for the ecclesiastically proper. We must form for prophetic presence, not for institutional development that insulates us from the life of others. We must form for the Torah rather than for a temple long gone and well dead.

The fact is that we do not have a vocation crisis. God never fails to "comfort the people." No, we do not have a vocation crisis; we have a crisis of spirituality and a crisis of significance. No vocation program in the world can make up for those.

And can we do it? Can a religious life shaken to its foundation by change come to life again? Oh, no doubt about it. The era speaks for itself. The fact is that we have been doing it for 30 long years, with little approval, limited understanding, small appreciation, and little certainty beyond the gospel, but the results are clear: when our own hearts are aflame, no effort is too much, no effort fails.

16.

Afterword: These Lives Ablaze

The Irish have another custom associated with *grieshog*. Besides burying the last hot ember of the day in cold coals overnight in order to start the next day's peat fire quickly, the Irish preserve the fire from home to home as well. When a young person marries or when the family moves, they take a hot coal from the first hearth to start the first fire in the new one. The Irish know that no fire lasts forever, that new fire has to come from somewhere, that fire is the energizing center of the home, that the fires that warmed us before are worthy to warm us in the future. They take something from the old hearth, in other words, to shape the quality of the fire in what is to be the new one. Religious life must do the same now if we are to pass on to a new century the best of this one.

We have not lost the virtues of the past; we have simply shaped them into ones necessary to our own times. Now we must own these new ones and form ourselves in them and carry them proudly. Religious life is not a life being betrayed in this period; it is a life being begun again, under the most difficult of circumstances, with the highest of motives and the most profound, the most brilliant of results. Religious of this period have repopulated the cities of the world with new services, with a new kind of presence, with new voice, with unflagging energy, with total trust and at great cost to themselves as people. Benefactors disappeared, critics decried them, membership declined, and, in some cases, even the church abandoned religious because, ironically, at the direction of the church, they followed the Spirit to the future rather than the past.

Is the transition complete? Absolutely not. There are miles yet to go up the mountain of decision. But the path is clearer now. There is a configuration of spiritual strength emerging that accounts for the gains of the immediate past period of renewal, and which, if it is recognized for what it is by congregations as a whole, promises even more vitality in the future. The one remaining obstacle, as I see it, lies in continuing to mourn what was and ignore the clear spiritual power of the present. Religious life has the opportunity at this time to be more religious than it ever imagined.

Contemplation is at the core of contemporary religious life. Congregations find themselves awash in the mystery of the God of motion. Steeped in charism and intent only on God, religious life is being called beyond spiritual formulas found tried and true in the past to the frightening depths of the God who goes on creating, even now, from nothing. Contemporary religious are called to the contemplation of God in time as few generations before them have been.

A conscious sense of purpose undergirds the ongoing development of contemporary religious life. Resurrection nibbles at the heels of religious life, dependent not only on trust in the God whom we know leads every seeking soul from Egypt to the Promised Land, but also on the continuing commitment to commitment that is required of the seeker. Part of the holiness of the religious life of our time lies precisely in the energy we bring to what appears to be dying.

The search for God in dailiness – the daily search for God – marks religious life as religious life, intent only on the conscious presence of God and the conscientious pursuit of God's Word, no matter what else must be surrendered for the sake of the search.

The ability to risk – as the Israelites risked over and over again in the trek through the desert – challenges religious life to the heights now. Nothing from the past is secure. Nothing in the future is clear. Risk is the new asceticism of religious life. Like the consequences of fasting and silence and detachment before it, the ability to try and fail brings religious of this time to the high point of trust in God. Risk is the virtue that builds the bridge between religious life now and religious life to come.

What diminishment does for contemporary religious life, the symbolic sacrifices of religion can only give hint. Loss of numbers, loss of institutions, loss of a sense of future, loss of a sense of accomplishment make a value a reality. Religious of this time do not have to talk "sacrifice," they are being called to live it.

To remain faithful when the whole world tells you not only that what you are doing in life is right but that to go on doing it is essential to your integrity is one thing. To remain faithful when you must ask yourself every day what you must do that is really religious is entirely another.

The virtue of contemporary religious life lies in the fact that there is very little except a vision of the highest nature to give fidelity to it at all. Fidelity now is not to a thing, to a person, not even to a way of life. The process of discernment itself is what measures religious fidelity now.

The cry for justice, personal responsibility and unlimited love demand a kind of virtue that dependence, docility and self-protection can never match for power, for struggle, for strain, for valor. The vowed life lives fresh and new in a world steeped in ruthless obedience, obscene poverty and gross human exploitations. The value of the vows of religion in contemporary society does not shine in what religious are against. The vitality of the vows of religion lives anew in this age only in those things that religious prove themselves to be for in the most holistic ways.

A commitment to the intellectual life, far beyond certification requirements or professional development, brings contemporary religious to the brink of ideas and their place in the gospel life. Contemporary religious virtue does not lie in piety alone, as inspiriting as piety is to the soul. The spirituality of a religious life lived in a period of never-ending questions depends for its authenticity on becoming a thinking presence, a credible voice for the reign of God.

Feminism, the spiritual art of developing a worldview based on humanity, dignity and equality for all, makes the Gospel real in a world suffering from the oppression of peoples, the rape of the land and the imbalance of soul in both church and state.

In the midst of all these shifts in values, structures and emerging philosophical insights, the proper question for religious life is not "What shall it become?" The question to which we must attend if religious life is ever to be anything at all in the future is, "What is it now?" There is no doubt about it. Contemporary religious life calls for great discipline, high virtue, a kind of holiness beyond the wildest imagination of those who came before us. Their search led to this one. Now our own commitment to the unformed but spiritually forming must make possible not only the next period of religious life but the quality of our own.

It is a changing time for religious life, but it is also an exciting one, a holy one. There is great fire in these ashes. All we need to do to fan the flame is to embrace the moment and live it to its cloud-shrouded summit. An ancient profession rite puts into the mouths of the newly-vowed candidates to religious life the chant: "Uphold me, O God, according to

Your word and I shall live. And do not fail me in my hope."
The question, of course, is for what did we hope when we
committed ourselves to such a way as this? For certainty? For
approval? For clarity? Surely the answer is far deeper than
that. Surely the answer must be the Gaelic one: if not to bank
the fire, then certainly to bury the coals, to carry them to new
places so that they can flame again. How else shall fire be
maintained in any period? Banking and burying coals are
simply different parts of the same process called the God-life,
called growing in commitment, in spirituality, in holiness –
in wisdom, age and grace. The only question now is whether
this generation, our generation, has yet the commitment, the
faith, the energy, the spiritual heat enough left for *grieshog*.
We are not the first generation for whom this is the content
of our lives, but unless we do it with all our hearts, another
generation may not get the opportunity to do the same, to
warm themselves at the same fire, to heat the world with the
coals of their lives.